P.S. Your Cat is Dead!

A COMEDY IN TWO ACTS

by James Kirkwood

SAMUEL FRENCH, INC.

25 WEST 45TH STREET   NEW YORK 10036
7623 SUNSET BOULEVARD   HOLLYWOOD 90046
LONDON   TORONTO

P.S. YOUR CAT IS DEAD! by James Kirkwood was performed at the Westwood Playhouse, Los Angeles, California from February 25 through March 28, 1976, under the direction of Milton Katselas. The play was produced by Margy Newman in association with Arthur Whitelaw, Michael L. Grace and Susan Bloom. Stage setting by Robert Zentis, lighting by Charles Schuman, costumes by David Graden and associate producer was Donald Phelps.

CHARACTERS
(*In Order of Appearance*)

VITO	*Jeff Druce*
KATE	*Claudette Nevins*
JIMMY	*Keir Dullea*
FRED	*William Jordan*
CARMINE	*Ronny Graham*
JANIE	*Roberta Callahan*
BOBBY	*Al Mancini*

P.S. YOUR CAT IS DEAD! by James Kirkwood, was first performed on April 7, 1975, at the John Golden Theatre in New York City. The play was produced by Richard Barr, Charles Woodward and Terry Spiegel in cooperation with the Buffalo Studio Arena Theatre under the direction of Vivian Matalon. Setting and lighting by William Ritman, costumes by Frank J. Boros, and associate producer was Neal Du Brock.

CHARACTERS
(*In Order of Appearance*)

VITO	*Tony Musante*
KATE	*Jennifer Warren*
JIMMY	*Keir Dullea*
FRED	*Peter White*
CARMINE	*Antony Ponzini*
JANIE	*Mary Hamill*
WENDELL	*Bill Moor*

SYNOPSIS OF SCENES

PLACE

Jimmy Zoole's loft apartment in New York City on New Year's Eve.

ACT ONE

SCENE 1: Late evening

SCENE 2: Thirty minutes later

ACT TWO

Later the same night

4

The time is the present. It is New Year's Eve.

Jimmy Zoole's loft-apartment is unusual in construction, being the third and top floor of an old factory building, about to be torn down, in the West Village over by the Hudson River, in the jumble of small jagged industrial streets that crowd that area.

The apartment has actually been constructed over a period of years out of a loft. The bathroom is the only separate room. A dandy kitchen, with a free standing butcher block sink unit, has been installed to be near the available plumbing—the reason for its not being up against a wall. Most of the walls have been stripped of plaster and are of old brick. One is still half-plastered. There is a large bed, raised somewhat on a platform (with enough room under the bed for someone to hide). Over the bed is a large skylight, which is practical and opens upward. This skylight and part of the adjoining roofs, heating or air-conditioning ducts or part of a chimney, should be seen above the set itself. There are two smaller skylights, no more than two-by-two feet, one over the bathroom area, the other over the kitchen. There is a small Christmas tree with lights on, placed on the desk or on the window sill. The furniture is comfortable and mixed; there is Jimmy's writing desk, a chaise, large throw cushions on the floor, book shelves, record cabinets, posters and pictures and other mementos that go toward making an individual home out of an apartment space in New York City. It has been done with pride and loving care, although it is not quite finished. And never will be.

CAST OF CHARACTERS

JIMMY ZOOLE: Attractive, thirty-eight-year-old actor who has not made it, but has not, so far, given up trying. In his attempts to achieve success he has kept himself as square as possible, that is— he has played the game according to the puritan ethic rules, jumped through the hoop, played "good dog" for about as long as one can play good dog without turning rabid. His sense of humor has often saved him from flipping out.

VITO ANTENUCCI: At twenty-seven he's been through more than his share of scrapes. Humpy, in an off-beat scroungy tom-cattish way, Vito would do and has done anything to get by. Despite a tacky life and his wiseguy toughness, he is an optimist, a parttime romantic and a soft touch. He is also a congenital fuck-up—but with flair and his own unique style.

KATE HOUGH: Pretty, sassy thirty-two-year-old liberated fashion photographer with a mind and a life-style of her own. A girl with very few hang-ups, she is candid and even opinionated, but not without warmth and caring.

FRED GABLE: Good-looking ad agency man in his mid-thirties, well-dressed, well-educated, thinks of himself as with-it, but is actually a bit *behind* it.

CRAZY CARMINE: Darkly handsome, volatile thirty-seven-year-old stage manager with pure libertine instincts. Carmine is a self-proclaimed, happily adjusted, totally dedicated sex maniac who would probably have it off with a kangaroo if it could be arranged without too much trouble.

6

JANIE: An attractive, vague, happy creature, an actress who takes more pleasure from being with her friends than from her career. Loves to give parties and to be included in the activities of others. Dizzy, off in another world most of the time.

BOBBY: Short, chunky, rugged fellow who aspires to the kinky. He has attached himself to Carmine like a pilot fish.

AUTHOR'S NOTES

Brief notes about *P.S. Your Cat Is Dead!* Because it was published as a novel in hardcover by Stein & Day and later by Warner's Paperback, some people assume *P.S.* was written as a novel first and then made into a play. I first wrote the story as a play; it was only while waiting for a production to materialize, that I began thinking in terms of a novel. I felt close to the story, I knew the characters well, so the book was written and published. The play has had a strange and un-orthodox history. It was first done at the Buffalo Studio Arena Theatre where it played a month's pre-Broadway engagement to completely sold-out houses. The Buffalo audiences took the play for what it was meant to be—an entertainment about two losers who meet at a certain crucial time in their lives. Will they help each other? The play also deals with the question: can we arrive at a point mid-way in our lives and change directions, if the career we've been pursuing is no longer satis-fying to us? I believe we can, if the desire to climb out of a rut is strong enough and there is sufficient will power to back up the scramble. I began as an actor and it was only after years as a performer that I began to write. And happily so, it turns out.

I was surprised at the reaction of some of the New York critics who found so much more in the play than was meant to be there. For instance, it is not a play proselytizing for bisexuality. Vito, the hustler-burglar, uses his sexuality as a commodity with which to trade in return for a place to stay, clothes, food and, most importantly, companionship. Some of the language is frankly rough, but Vito is a street person and to have him speak any other way would be false; four letter words are not sprinkled in for shock value or local color. The character of Kate is in no way the result of an anti-feminist mind. She is not a villainess. She is bright, warm and perky—if opinionated. It is only because she believes their affair has reached the point of diminishing returns that she leaves Jimmy, knowing if their relationship continues they will surely be in-flicting small hurts and punishments upon each other with in-creasing regularity. It is only out of affection for him that she tells him what she believes is wrong with his life.

8

The two leading characters, Jimmy and Vito, should both be played with utmost humor; it is this quality that enables them to get by as well as they do. They must be warm and vulnerable; if the audience does not have a love affair with both of them, the play is damaged. Most of all, it is a play to have fun with and Jimmy and Vito are characters that should touch the audience. I doubt there are few people walking around who, at one time or another, have not thought of themselves as losers. This should be the common denominator that makes the audience root for them.

The script, as published here, is the result of not only the New York production directed by Vivián Matalon with tender loving care, but of two other productions, one in San Francisco, the other in Los Angeles, the latter two directed with incredible energy and enthusiasm by Milton Katselas, to whom I am extremely indebted. It was Milton who nudged me into extensive rewrites, all of which made this a better play. I am also indebted to all the actors and actresses who have appeared in the productions so far for their contributions which have been considerable. A word of thanks also goes to Arthur Whitelaw who picked the play up immediately after it's New York run for production on the West Coast. No matter what, I do not consider this a critics' play, but then we don't write solely for the critics; we write for audiences and in the four cities in which this cat has played, the audiences have been warmly and openly responsive.

I hope whoever does *P.S. Your Cat Is Dead!* in the future will find this to be true.

Finally, this play is dedicated to Sal Mineo, who was a perfect Vito in San Francisco and who was rehearsing again for the Los Angeles production at the time of his tragic death. He is greatly missed.

9

P.S. Your Cat Is Dead!

ACT ONE

SCENE 1

*Loud jazz music [instrumental] plays as the lights
dim. The music continues, gradually fading out
by the time* VITO *pries open the skylight.* VITO
appears on the roof, extreme S. L., *over a darkened
loft apartment. He checks it out with a flashlight.
He crosses* R. *to a small vent, shines the light
through, crosses further* R. *to the large skylight,
shines the light through that, then pries the skylight open with a large screwdriver. He climbs
inside, surveys the drop to the bed below, and
says:*

VITO. Holy Shit! (*He drops his airline bag onto the
bed, grabs onto a pipe under the skylight, and swings,
finally letting himself drop to the bed. He pulls out
a gun from one pocket and a flashlight from another,
surveys the room, flashing out the contents: TV, cassette player, etc. He goes into the kitchen area,
searches with his flashlight, shines it upon crock-jar.
He lifts lid off, rummages down inside, only comes up
with a cookie. He cocks his head, looking at it, says:*)
Fuckin' cookie! (*Then pops it into his mouth. He
crosses to the desk,* U. S. C., *in front of the window,
and grabs cassette; he then rushes with it* D. S. *to the
TV, on a bench below the bed. He unplugs the TV,
grapples with it, cassette, gun and flashlight in hands,
muttering. He then puts the gun down between two
stacks of magazines on the bench, picks up the TV
and cassette easily, and tiptoes to the entrance land-*

11

*ing where he deposits them, near the small stereo set.
He hears noises in the hallway outside the front door.)*
Oh, shit . . . (*He runs to the bed, snatches his flightbag, douses the flashlight and jumps into the closet,
U. S. R. of bed as* KATE HOUGH *enters through front
door, extreme S. R., wearing coat and carrying purse,
keyring and suitcase. She closes the door behind her,
steps to the light switch and turns on LIGHT for
S. R. She walks to the bed, puts her suitcase down on
it, notices her fur coat lying on the bed, picks it up,
looks around, confused as to why it's there, puts it
down, then crosses L. to the Onstage side of the sink
unit. She switches on KITCHEN LIGHTS. She puts
down her purse, crosses back to the bed and sheds her
coat. She walks toward closet as: the TELEPHONE
RINGS and interrupts her from quite going into
closet. She crosses to the sink unit, to the telephone
on D. S. end, hesitates, and then answers.)*

KATE. (*At the sink, using a fake accent.*) Allo,
Buenas dias! . . . (*Then, natural voice.*) Oh, uh, no,
he isn't. . . . Yes, wait a second . . . (*Locating a pen
and pad on shelf of sink unit.*) Yes, go ahead . . . Oh,
the animal hospital . . . Sure, yes, his . . . Oh, no,
not his *cat! Oh, Bobby Seale is dead!* (VITO *peeks out
of the closet.*) . . . Oh, Lord, he just adored that
mangy cat . . . No, I'm just on my way out, I'll leave
him a note and have him call *you.* Yes, thank you.
Goodbye. (*Hangs up phone.*) Oh, Lord-God-Almighty!
You really know how to pull 'em, don't you? (*Reaching into her purse, taking out an envelope, holding it
up and talking to herself, paraphrasing the contents.*)
"Dear Jimmy, Well, we tried, but it just didn't work
out. So I'm leaving you. I wish you a long happy suc-
cessful life. Love and kisses—Kate. P.S. Happy New
Year. *P.P.S. Your cat is dead!* (*Propping the envelope
on the telephone dial.*) Well, onward and downward.
(*Walking toward bathroom door.*) Hit 'em when
they're down. (*Exits into bathroom. The BATH-*

ROOM LIGHT goes on. VITO creeps from closet and hurries toward the outside door. He hears approaching footsteps outside, mutters "Shit!," turns back and scrambles under the L. side of bed. JIMMY ZOOLE enters, disheveled, wearing short trench coat, and closes door behind him, muttering to himself unintelligably. He doffs his coat and lays it on the chaise; he sits on the hassock, C. [One Beat] KATE enters from bathroom, with toilet articles, mirror, etc. in both hands.) Jimmy! *(She stops in her tracks.)*

JIMMY. Oh, Kate! Ah—I thought we were spending New Year's apart. *(He rises, walks to KATE.)* Oh, Lady—am I ever glad to see you. *(Puts his arms around her.)* Am I ever! *(KATE does not respond; JIMMY pulls away, sees what she holds in her hands, then the suitcase.)* I think I am . . .

KATE. *(Walks to S. L. of bed.)* I thought you were going right up to Claire's.

JIMMY. I was, but something came up. I decided to . . . I take it you're going someplace, too. *(KATE does not reply.)* Well, aren't you? *(No reply.) Aren't you?*

KATE. *(Quietly.)* Yes.

JIMMY. *(Hit hard.)* Yes. Yes . . . Well— Oh, boy, yeah . . . Great . . . Nifty . . . Neat . . . *(He pauses, spots the TV and Cassette on entrance platform S. R. He walks toward them.)* Look, I don't mind you taking back your own Christmas present, but *I* bought the cassette.

KATE. *(Pained.)* I *gave* you the TV for Christmas. What a terrible thing to say! I wasn't taking either one of them.

JIMMY. What—they've got dates for New Year's Eve? *(Picking up the TV and cassette and speaking to the two pieces.)* You two stepping out again? I thought I told you about that . . .

KATE. *(Going below bed to closet.)* Don't be ridiculous!

JIMMY. I'm not in the habit of unplugging them and setting them by the door every time I go out.

KATE. (*Taking a dress out of the closet.*) I told you I wasn't taking them. Don't you believe me?

JIMMY. No, I don't believe you. (*Takes TV and cassette and places them on bench* D. S. *of bed, as* KATE *crosses down from closet.*)

KATE. Oh, well I . . .

JIMMY. (*Walking to telephone* D. S. *end of sink.*) Well, whaddaya know, the mailman's been here! (*Picks up envelope.*)

KATE. (*Walking toward him.*) No, Jimmy, don't— not now!

JIMMY. Christ, it's addressed to me, isn't it?

KATE. (*Following him.*) I know, but you've been drinking.

JIMMY. (*Moving to get away from her.*) Hurray— the news flashes are coming in. Stop the presses! "He's been drinking."

KATE. Jimmy, please don't . . .

JIMMY. Please don't! You— For God's sake, you're leaving, obviously you're leaving. This is obviously —a Dear John, and you don't want me to *open* it! Who knows, I might even have a reply for once!

KATE. I'd rather you read it after . . . (*Trying to reach around him for letter which he holds away from her.*)

JIMMY. Well, you've been out-voted. (*He opens the unsealed envelope and reads:*) "Dear Jimmy"— Well, so far so good. It's not a laugh riot, but—you know, it's got a nice *homey* touch!

KATE. Stop it!

JIMMY. (*Putting letter back into envelope and licking it closed.*) I cannot wait! (*He slams the envelope down on the sink.*) *The suspense is absolutely killing me!*

KATE. You said you were going right up to Claire's

from rehearsals. How did I know you weren't? How did I—

JIMMY. How did I know I was going to be *fired!* (*Walks to chaise and sits.*) I'm sorry, my plans changed. I—

KATE. Jimmy! (*Going to him.*) Oh, Jimmy! Oh, angel . . .

JIMMY. I just didn't feel like rushing up there and putting on a paper hat. (*Turning away from her.*)

KATE. Jimmy— I had no idea. Oh, Jimmy, I'm so sorry! (*Embraces him; he does not respond.*) Jimmy?

JIMMY. Get away—please! I really don't want to cry, not in front of Miss Strength and Guts, not in front of our Lady Photographer. (*Fending her off.*) If you maul me, I will! (*Rises.*) Please! (*Walking away from her.*)

KATE. And what would you be crying about? Would it be *me* or the job?

JIMMY. Oh, terrific! Can't I just play it across the board? Do I *have* to pick a category? (KATE *laughs.*) What's so funny?

KATE. You. I always did get a kick out of you, when you got mad.

JIMMY. Whoopee! (*Then after a beat, crossing* U. S. *to desk.*) You know what I hate the most? I was all set to get up every morning and be able to go to work— (*Picking up script from desk.*) to *do* my work. Now there's no reason to—even get out of bed in the morning. (*Dumping script into wastebasket next to desk.*)

KATE. Jimmy, I'm so sorry about the play. But why . . . ?

JIMMY. The why? You won't *believe* the why! Miss Hollywood Star wanted her boyfriend to play my part in the first place, but he was starting a picture in Spain. Yesterday, he got into an argument with the director, that English Sir Waldo-what's-his-name, on the set, in front of the entire cast and crew, and called him "a dizzy cunt!" (*Giving it a camp reading.*) "What was *that?*" asked Sir Waldo. He repeated it, with embellishments. Sir Waldo kicked him off the picture, (*Going to refrigerator* s. L.) boyfriend phones Miss Hollywood Star, and she laid the word down to the producers. Know what gets me? (*Walking to sink with ice tray.*) Some flipped-out actor calls a director a "dizzy cunt" in *Madrid*—and *I* get fired in New York!

KATE. Rotten—it's rotten.

JIMMY. (*Walking to refrigerator for ice bucket.*) Well, we agree on something. But stay tuned for the rest of the news. (*Back to the sink.*) The soap opera's kaput, too.

KATE. Kaput?

JIMMY. (*Filling ice bucket.*) Kaput!

KATE. I thought they were just writing you out while the play was out of town.

JIMMY. (*Filling icetray with water from sink faucet.*) The ratings have been way down lately, so they made one *little* change in the storyline. (*Going to refrigerator with icetray.*) Instead of writing me off on that two-month expedition up the Amazon, from which they were going to bring me back with some mysterious disease, (*Back to the sink.*) they've decided to—just let me *drown* in the goddam Amazon!

KATE. But, Jimmy, I thought you signed a three-year contract.

JIMMY. (*Filling two glasses with ice.*) It can be cancelled every thirteen weeks.

KATE. So how can it be a three-year contract?

JIMMY. The network can cancel, but not the performer.

KATE. Great! What kind of clause is that?

JIMMY. We call that— The Fuck-You Clause.

KATE. Uh-huh . . . Acting—what a tacky business!

JIMMY. (*Taking hold of* KATE, *crowding her backwards up against sink.*) At least it solves our problem, doesn't it? You won't have to put up with all of that jazz: No more soap opera, no more learning lines every night, no more working on the book, even. Now we can really play house!

KATE. Jimmy, stop it!

JIMMY. That's what you objected to, wasn't it? I couldn't go out at night, I couldn't play, I couldn't . . .

KATE. No-o-o-o, that wasn't what I objected to at all— (*Breaks his grip and walks to the bed.*) Oh, this is ridiculous!

JIMMY. Want a drink?

KATE. No, thanks. (*Resumes packing.*)

JIMMY. Mind if I do? *Mind if I do!* It's my house, it's my liquor— What the hell am I talking about! (*Pours himself a drink.*)

KATE. Go ahead— (*Walking toward bathroom door.*) I'll be leaving in a minute. (*Going into bathroom.*)

JIMMY. (*Quickly goes to stereo, pulls out LP from bin below it, slips record from jacket.*) Come on, Richard, do your stuff! (*Puts it on turntable, flicks switch to play record. The RECORD PLAYS. Richard Harris: "Didn't We?" JIMMY quickly moves U. S. C., below desk. KATE enters from bathroom L. with hair brush and cosmetic bag in hands. JIMMY grabs her to dance to:*)

VOICE. (*Richard Harris.*) "This time we almost made the pieces fit, didn't we, girl?"

JIMMY.   (*Singing—*) Didn't we, girl?

(*They dance. JIMMY takes brush from KATE's hand and drops in sink; ditto cosmetic bag.*)

VOICE. (*Richard Harris.*) "This time we almost made some sense of it, didn't we, girl?"

JIMMY.   (*Singing—*) Didn't we, girl?

KATE. You're being mean.

JIMMY. *I'm* being mean? Who's walking out on who New Year's Eve?

KATE. (*Breaking away from him.*) I picked tonight because I knew you'd be at Claire's, also because I thought you'd be so tied up with the play it wouldn't matter that much.

JIMMY. Oh, Kate!

KATE. (*Picking up brush and bag from sink.*) Oh, *come on*, Jimmy! It's not as if it were news. We both knew it was coming to this. We said we'd skip New Years and—

JIMMY. You said, you said, *you* said! You were the one who said we'd spend New Years apart. You were invited, same as last year.

KATE. To sit around with that back-biting aunt of yours and watch her dangle you on a string? (*Groans, walking to stereo.*) "You're my only family, Jimmy, and when I die . . ." and on and on. Promises, promises. (*Taking the tone arm off record.*) Wind the Aunt Claire Doll up and it promises to die!

JIMMY. Let's not get into that again.

KATE. (*Moving back toward* JIMMY.) Because it's the worst possible form of blackmail; it's disgusting and demeaning. And you know it. I can tell by your face when you sit there and listen to all that anti-talk. Anti-the-Blacks, anti-the-Jews, anti-the-Catholics. God, she's probably *anti-histamine!* But you sit there and—doesn't it make you feel dirty? (*Pause;* JIMMY *looks away.*) Okay, no reply needed. You know what the annoying thing is about you?

JIMMY. You mean there's *some one thing* you haven't told me?

KATE. Yes, about a dozen, if you really want to know.

JIMMY. I don't.

KATE. Good, I'll tell you. You're thirty-eight years old, and maybe you're really a good actor— I mean *could be* if . . .

JIMMY. That's the most encouraging thing you've ever said. Thanks.

KATE. De Nada. But you play it so almighty safe! All right, I'm going to tell you something else . . .

JIMMY. (*Turning away from her.*) Oh, Jesus!

KATE. Yes, well, oh Jesus, I am. Two people were talking about you at a party once, and one of 'em said, "That Jimmy Zoole, he's such an attractive guy. Say, are his front teeth capped?" Do you know what the other one said? *"Jimmy Zoole's whole life is capped!"*

JIMMY. (*Laughs, then does a take.*) What's that supposed to mean?

KATE. What? It means you have absolutely no imagination, not a fresh idea in your head about how to present yourself. You should—I dunno—mix it up. You—ought to—tell off the director when he gives you a hard time, or walk out of one of those cattle-call auditions when they make you wait three hours. But you're always so busy playing *Good Dog* for everybody; you roll over, sit up and bark. (*Resumes packing.*) An actor? You conduct yourself like some dried-up ad agency squeak!

JIMMY. Because I'm an actor I should be swinging from tree to tree like Tarzan? Beating my chest and raping everything in sight? Acting's not some parttime hobby. It's a business like any other.

KATE. You know what I mean; you won't even take chances with the parts you're offered.

JIMMY. Oh, that again. I don't want the first movie I make— I don't want to be standing on a cliff in Technicolor and Panavision with my three-piece-set blowing in the wind.

KATE. (*Going to him.*) Oh, stop it! You were very excited about it. It was about a man about to commit suicide, not about a guy standing on a cliff exposing himself—but that's what you turned it into, when it got down to the line. Oh, no, not Mr. Caution. You cling to the safe things: That tired soap, your occasional summer tour in—God help us—*Mary, Mary!*

JIMMY. Sorry, I'm not that much in demand. I don't get offered every choice role that comes along on Broadway, you know.

KATE. Then you must be doing *something* wrong! For God's sake, Jimmy, you're attractive, you're a—

JIMMY. *And you're an all-American, three-dimensional, supreme pain in the ass!* (*Lies down on throw-pillows* D. S. C.)

KATE. Funny, that's just what my horoscope said today. Let's leave it at that, shall we? (*Walks to the bed, begins to zip her packed suitcase.*) I've dropped my bomb, and like any sensible bomber, I'll leave. (*Wheeling, stepping toward* JIMMY.) And one more stupid thing: Two consenting adults, in 1975, keeping separate apartments. How really colossally dumb! And don't think I don't know why; (JIMMY *flops on his belly, focusing out.*) Aunt Claire would have changed her will again if we'd actually lived together. Her *will*—she's just the type to string everybody along for ninety years, and then leave it all to a Home for Unwed Canaries!

JIMMY. (*Shouting.*) Stop it, stop it, stop it! Level with me, do you have *one,* just *one,* unuttered opinion?

KATE. Uhhhhhh, no—I guess I don't. (*Walking to sink unit.*) Oh, what the heck. One for the breakup. (*Pouring whiskey into setup glass.*) Here's to the good times. We had some rocky ones. (*Going to him.*) But we had some good ones, too. Funny, for anyone as basically old-fashioned, filled-to-the-brim with the Puritan Ethic, you really do make the wildest huggle-bunnyburgers.

JIMMY. (*Laughing.*) Jesus, that is brutal. Who made that up? Did you?

KATE. No, my angel, you did. (*Sitting on throw-pillows.*) Actually, I've grown rather fond of it.

JIMMY. *Hugglebunnyburgers!* Uck! (*Then.*) Were they really that good?

KATE. (*Stretching out next to him.*) Tops in town. Actually, I think that's what hooked me on you, least at first. I mean when we'd be out, you're so—oh, opening doors, Boy Scoutish, helping old women and blind people across streets, never giving a cab driver back any of the lip they give out. Then we'd get home and . . . Wow, it was like some dusty Italian workman.

JIMMY. Yeah?

KATE. Yeah. I remember one afternoon, the time you bounced us right off the bed, and then we just concluded right there on the floor. That evening, we went to a cocktail party; lots of theatrical people there. You were so nervous, your hand would tremble ever-so-slightly when you'd reach for a drink. I remember thinking back a couple of hours earlier when you were behaving like a caveman, and I thought, hmnnnn . . . Maybe Jimmy ought to treat the whole world a little more like, well—

JIMMY. Like what?

KATE. Like he was screwing it.

JIMMY. Enchanting.

KATE. Jimmy, all those unuttered opinions were uttered . . . because I care about you. Don't you know that? Listen, I realize it's a sore point, but I hope you'll get back to your book. It was so good.

JIMMY. To start all over again! It's hard to get steam up.

KATE. But please don't give up on it, just because—

JIMMY. (*Taking her hand.*) Let's not talk about that now. Listen, you can move your things back to your place, but—why don't we spend New Year's together? I'll call Claire up and tell her I can't make it.

KATE. No, I can't, Jimmy. Honestly, I—if I'd known that all this, I mean—but it was agreed we'd spend New Year's apart and—well, I made other plans.

JIMMY. (*Letting go of her hand.*) Plans . . .

KATE. Yes.

JIMMY. Oh, you made *plans*. Well, that's different. Plans, huh? Would these be *Johnnie* Plans? Or *Joe* Plans?

KATE. I'm—we're going to a party tonight, then tomorrow up to Vermont for some skiing, just for the day.

JIMMY. You mean you made a date with some guy, then you suggested we skip New Year's so—

KATE. No, it didn't happen like that! (*Rising, going to sink.*) Please, give me that much credit. (*Putting her glass down.*)

JIMMY. Please my ass! No wonder Claire was catching such hell. You had to dump it on someone. You're probably in the middle of your next affair! (*Up on his knees.*) Why the hell didn't you just tell me, instead of letting me beg and . . .

KATE. It's just someone I met through work, and he asked me and I—

JIMMY. (*Rising.*) And you just— Oh, shit, get out!

KATE. Jimmy, stop it! (*Walking to the bed.*)

JIMMY. (*Going to the sink.*) Get out!

KATE. (*Picks up coat from bed and begins to put it on.*) I will, *I will!*

JIMMY. (*Grabs letter from sink, rips it to pieces and scatters them over his head.*) Christ, I'd rather read the entire collected works of Harold Robbins! (*He steps into bathroom;* KATE *picks up her shoulderbag;* JIMMY *returns, brandishing a plastic case.*) Here— you'd better take your *equipment!* (KATE *takes the diaphragm case automatically;* JIMMY *goes to the front door.*)

KATE. (*Tossing diaphragm case on bed.*) Keep it, I won't be needing it. I bought a new one. (*Picks up her suitcase and fur coat.*)

JIMMY. Enchanting! Just like you to say that. Get out. (*He jerks open the outside door.*)

KATE. (*Walking toward the door.*) Goodbye. I'm sorry we had to have this little squabble.

JIMMY. If you'd just been honest with me from the beginning, we wouldn't have. What a dirty, sneaky, low-down—

KATE. Enchanting! (*Exiting.*) Goodbye!

JIMMY. (*Yelling out the door.*) Good luck! (*Leaning out.*) As we say in the theatre, break a leg! Break both of them! That way you'll have an excuse for staying on your *back!* (*He slams the door, steps away, then yanks it open and shouts out:*) Mazeltov! (*Slams door again. Looking around, he then rushes to the bed, snatches up diaphragm, runs to the window, opens it, and hurls the diaphragm out. Shouts:*) Lacheim! May all your orgasms turn to stone! (*Turns around, walks D. S., spots bowl of fruit, runs to sink unit, grabs bowl and hurries back to window where he throws three pieces of fruit out and down.*) Here you go— Hey! Hah! That's right, hustle it up! Your precious little Jimmy must be flipping! Oops!—almost gotcha! Wheee! (*Giggling.*) Dropped her goddam fur coat! (*Rushes back to the refrigerator, grabs a head of lettuce and a tomato, tears back to the window.*) Here yah go, baby—have a little salad! *Tossed* salad— natch! (*Giggles, tosses it out the window.*) Farewell, my little hummingbird—don't take any wooden hugglebunnyburgers! (*JIMMY closes the window, walks D. S. to end of bed platform.*) Jesus, maybe I am flipping. (*Spots himself in mirror S. L.*) Happy New Year—Dumb-ass. Jesus, some New Year! (*Crosses to C.*) So—well— Life is a shit sandwich, and every day we have to take another bite. (*Crosses below bench, D. S. bed.*) Who said that? Yeah, but this is pure gluttony. (*JIMMY sits on the magazine stacks on the bench; jumps up and pulls out gun from between stacks; looks quickly around as if to find the answer to this mystery.*) Maybe they're trying to tell me something. (*Looks up, gun in hand.*) Are you trying to tell me something? Huh? (*Shudders.*) Spooky . . . Very spooky. Now *this is spooky!* (*JIMMY points the gun off* S. R. *and pulls trigger; it clicks only. The TELEPHONE RINGS.* JIMMY *jumps, startled; rises, one hand to his heart.* JIMMY *walks to sink and telephone.*) Hello . . . Oh, Claire— (*Leaning on sink.*) I was just going to call you . . . Claire, I'm sorry, but I can't come up. . . . No, it's just— Listen, can I level with you, and will you try to understand? . . . Good . . . No, I'm not spending it with Kate . . . Claire, you haven't let me *explain* . . . No, I'm not sick, but I'm . . . Claire, for God's sake, stop talking a second and listen! . . . All right, that's better. Look, I've had a really bad day. I got—Claire, I'm not *finished!* Jesus, you just refuse to *listen!* (*Slams the phone down.*) Pussy! *Deaf Goddam Pussy!* (JIMMY *walks to hassock, sits; immediately. The TELEPHONE RINGS.* JIMMY *hurries to sink, puts telephone on floor* D. S. R. *sink, kneels* S. R. *of it and pantomimes "shooting" it with the gun, then pantomimes a huge mushroom cloud rising above the phone as a result of his imaginary explosion. The phone continues ringing and he answers it.*) Hello . . . I know it's not like me, but I made my point, didn't I? . . . Look, I've been fired from the play, I'm being written out of the soap, Kate's walked out, my cat's sick with a kidney infection, I'm thirty-eight years old and I've been robbed two times in the last three months—and one little thing you didn't know— I was writing a novel, and as far as I'd gotten, 162 pages, was in a small metal box and *that* was taken in the last robbery. I am deeply depressed. Happy New Year! (*He hangs up.*) Deaf old witch! (JIMMY *walks a few steps away, then spins around, aiming the gun at the phone.*) Go ahead, ring. See if I care. (*The TELEPHONE RINGS.*) Ring away. Ring your *bells* off. Ring till *Doomsday!* (*Then.*) Christ, that's today! (JIMMY *fires at the telephone while backing* D. R.: *gun fires on fourth try.* JIMMY *falls back, almost to the floor, braces himself with one hand.*)

VITO. Jesus! (*He slides out* L. *of bed; duffle bag gets caught under bed; he tugs at it, trying to get it out.*)

JIMMY. What? Who's—what the—?

VITO. (*Hands up.*) Okay, don't do nothin'. Don't do nothin' now! (JIMMY *opens his mouth to speak, but no words come out.*) Take it easy! Take it easy! Okay, it's a draw! Just let me outta here. (*Leaving bag, he moves stealthily toward front door.*)

JIMMY. (*Aiming the gun at* VITO.) Let you out! What the—who the hell *are* you?

VITO. Forget it, there was only one bullet!

JIMMY. Where the—where did you *come from?*

VITO. Keep the gun—it's empty.

JIMMY. (*Firing the empty gun at* VITO.) Who are you?

VITO. The Avon Lady— (*He heads for the door;* JIMMY *throws the gun toward the bed and is after him.* VITO *gets door open.*) So long and good luck!

JIMMY. (*Rushing to the door, grabbing* VITO, *pulling him down.*) You—fucking robber! (*Getting* VITO *down on floor.*) You son-of-a-bitch!

. VITO. Jesus, what is this— Quit it! Quit it! Let me outta here!

JIMMY. Let you outta here! Why, you dirty bastard! You—

VITO. (*Gagging.*) Hey, quit it. Jesus— Uncle, I give up! Quit it! (VITO *gets one leg up, rolls* JIMMY *off and scrambles toward Center Stage.*)

JIMMY. (*Follows, gets* VITO *in head lock and rolls* D. S.) Quit it? Why should I quit it—you no good dirty bastard!

VITO. For the main reason—it hurts!

JIMMY. (*Straddling* VITO, *beginning to strangle him.*) Good! Good! You miserable son-of-a-bitch!

VITO. Quit it! Quit it! Jesus. Help—help! Hey, wait a minute—your cat's dead! Your *goddam cat's dead!*

JIMMY. (*Stops dead, sitting atop* VITO.) What! What do you mean? *My cat!*

VITO. (*Quickly.*) Your lady-friend, she got a phone call from the cat hospital!

JIMMY. *Cat* hospital?

VITO. Cat hospital—dog hospital—what do you want? *Animal* hospital. Anyhow, the fuckin' cat's dead! (*Slips out from under* JIMMY *and heads toward far side of sink.*)

JIMMY. (*Lunging at him again.*) Why you son-of a-bitch!

VITO. Hey, cool it, cool it, I didn't kill it! (*Grabs ice bucket from sink to hurl.*)

JIMMY. What are you doing here? Jesus, I'll bet you're the same bastard that robbed me before! (*Grabs broom* U. S. *sink unit, hits at* VITO *across sink;* VITO *holds up ice bucket as shield.*) Are you? *Are you?*

VITO. (*Ducking back.*) No. No, and I wouldn't now. (*Slamming down bucket on counter.*) Honest, not after what I heard— (VITO *jumps sink toward bed;* Fight sequence: JIMMY *catches* VITO D. S. L. *end of bed; spins* VITO *around, wrestles him down on the bed with* VITO's *back to audience, on knees;* JIMMY *hits him in the stomach;* VITO *doubles over.* JIMMY *holds him up by the collar for more.*) Jesus, take it easy! What are you—crazy?

JIMMY. Crazy?

VITO. Help! Jesus, help, help!

JIMMY. (*Giving* VITO *a haymaker punch to the jaw.*) I'll show you crazy!

VITO. (*Staggering backwards.*) Ahhh! (VITO *stumbles backwards, across the hassock, crashes to the floor, knocked out and silent.* JIMMY *comes to stand over him.*)

JIMMY. (*Shouting.*) I got him, I got him! (*Runs to window, opens it and calls out to no one inparticular.*) I caught him, I got him! I— (JIMMY *rushes to chaise, picks up his coat, starts putting it on as he rushes to the front door, opens it, races out, slamming it behind him; immediately the door opens and he runs back in, taking his coat off.*) What am I doing? (*Goes to the phone, picks it up, dials operator.*) Hello, operator, what's the police emergency number? . . . 911, thank you. (*He dials 911, glancing down at the burglar. No answer, for a long time.* JIMMY *begins pacing back and forth behind* VITO, *every-now-and-then glancing at the receiver. Finally, out of patience:*) Come on, come on! Police emergency, my ass! (*Waiting for the phone to be answered, he looks down again at* VITO, *then slowly hangs up the phone.*) Oh, no. No, no, no. Un-uh. Ah . . . ah . . . ? (*Glances around, pantomimes rope, tugging a rope.*) Where's the . . . ah . . . ? (*Dashes to the desk, looks through it: nothing; again pantomimes rope.*) Ah . . . ah . . . (*Runs to the sink and takes out a length of rope from beneath it, goes to* VITO. *As* JIMMY *picks up* VITO's *arms to tie his hands together:*)

BLACKOUT—MUSIC UP LOUD

ACT ONE

SCENE 2

MUSIC FADES. LIGHTS UP. The telephone is D. S. *of sink.* VITO *is strapped, bellydown, to the large butcher block sink unit. His hands are tied to towel-ring* D. S. *end of sink, his feet are tied together and three different strap-arrangements, from his upper back to his calves, go around his body and are hooked under the sink unit or passed completely through it. He is just coming to. He stirs his head, tries to move his body, can't, perceives his predicament, struggles mightily at first, then less as he realizes he is tied down securely.*

VITO. Jesus, what is this—the end of the world?
(*Calling out, turning his head.*) Hey, hey— *What's-*
your-name! Hey, ah— Jimmy . . . Yeah, hey Jimmy!
(*Shouting.*) Hey—hey, Jim-may! (*Turns his head the
other way.*) Hey—where the hell is everybody? (*A
pause; he mutters.*) Oh, Vito-baby, you done it again.
Alla-time, three lemons. Pong, pong, pong! (*Sighs.*)
New Year's Eve, too. Jesus! (*Footsteps are heard outside door. The door opens.* JIMMY *enters, carrying
groceries in a bag, closes the door, doesn't lock it.*)
Hey, what'd you tie me down for? Huh? Answer me,
what'd you go and tie me down for? Huh? Hey, you
didn't call the cops, did you? Did you? (*JIMMY flashes
him a huge grin, then walks to the kitchen, sets the
groceries down on counter unit.*) Listen, I got twenty-
seven bucks in my pocket— (*Glances around, suddenly aware his coat is off.*) Hey, you took my coat
off. You can have that, and I got two ounces of stuff,
cleaned, really good stuff, the strongest, (*JIMMY walks
to the bed and doffs coat.*) Senegalese Thunderfuck,
they call it. (*JIMMY goes back to the kitchen.*) Come
on, guy, I didn't do nothin' to you. (*JIMMY unloads
bag onto counter, opens bottle of champagne, gets
glass.*) Hey, how long you gonna keep me here? Come
on, guy, give a guy a break! It's New Year's Eve!
(*The cork pops.* VITO *mutters:*) Whoopee. Your eyes.
(JIMMY *walks* D. S. L. *of chaise and drinks from glass.*)
Yeah, and my ass! (*JIMMY continues drinking.*) Hey,
what about me— I'm thirsty. Even in jail they give
you a lousy drink! (*No reply.*) Hey, guy. I'm goddam
thirsty! (*JIMMY pours a second glass of champagne.*)
Hey, whaddya know, the warden ain't so bad after—
(JIMMY *walks toward* VITO, *flicking the champagne
in his face; then empties last drops over his head.*)
Jesus! What is it with you! You nut! Wouldn't I have
to get mixed up with a goddam nut! (*JIMMY returns to
the kitchen and continues unpacking bag.*) Okay, joke
over. (*JIMMY sets up folding butler's tray with dishes,*

candle-stick and flatware.) You had your kicks. So you caught me, but I didn't take nothin'. Let me up, let me outta here. What? You're not talkin' to me, huh? You beat the shit outta me, knock me the fuck out, tie me up—and *you're not talkin' to me!* BFD— Big Fuckin' Deal. (*A beat.*) I shouldn't be talkin' to *you!* (*A pause.*) Is that the big scoop? You're not talkin' to me?

(*The TELEPHONE RINGS.*)

JIMMY. (*Picking up telephone, walking away from* VITO, *toward chaise.*) Hello . . . Oh, hi, Kate, I remember you. Big eyes, big *mouth.* Didn't we used to . . . Yeah . . . Yes, I'm okay . . .

VITO. (*Shouting.*) Help! Help! I'm tied up, this crazy— (JIMMY *quickly goes to* VITO, *holds the receiver to his mouth.* VITO *does a take, looks at receiver, at* JIMMY, *back at receiver, then speaks in stunned normal voice.*) this crazy . . . nut has me tied up . . . help, goddamit . . . help.

JIMMY. (*Nodding, smiling, walking away from him.*) That? . . . Oh, that's some ratty little crum-bum burglar I caught. Yes, in the apartment, where else? . . . I'm not kidding!

VITO. (*Shouting.*) He's not kidding, goddamit! Help me! Help!

JIMMY. (*Into phone.*) Yes, I'm serious . . . who do you think that is, Claire? . . . Oh, the television? . . . (*To* VITO, *holding the receiver out to him.*) She thinks you're the telly!

VITO. (*Shouting.*) Fuckin' nut!

JIMMY. (*Into phone.*) Kate, they don't say "fuckin'" on TV . . . I don't know, how would I know? . . . (*To* VITO.) What's your name?

VITO. None of your fuckin' business!

JIMMY. (*Into phone.*) Hold on a second. . . . (*Puts phone down, gets skillet from pillar, runs some water*

into skillet, holds it as if to dump it on VITO's *head.*)
Or would you prefer it *hot?*

VITO. Okay, okay . . . Vito!

JIMMY. Vito what?

VITO. Vito Antonucci.

JIMMY. (*Empties skillet in sink under* VITO.) That's
better, and careful the way you talk to me. Remember.
you're not actually sitting in the catbird seat. (*Puts
fry pan on pillar* U. S. *of sink.*)

VITO. Huh?

JIMMY. Forget it, dumb-ass! (*Picks up phone.*)
Name's Vito . . . Oh, who knows? I may castrate
him . . . (VITO *reacts.*) or chop him up in little pieces,
wrap him in newspaper and deposit him in various
garbage cans around the city. Remember when that
sort of thing was in vogue? . . . No, I'm fine . . .
Well, you call me when you get back from skiing and
I'll let you know the final results . . . Oh, and watch
that last jump, it's a bitch!

VITO. (*Shouting.*) Help!

JIMMY. (*Into the phone.*) And may your New Year's
be just as kicky as mine. Mr. *Square* signing off, over
and out!

VITO. (*As* JIMMY *hangs up.*) Help!

JIMMY. (*Puts phone on chaise, walks to kitchen.*)
Vito Antonucci. Hmnn, I never did trust Germans.
(*Gets plate and places on top of counter.*)

VITO. Whack-oh fruitcake! Eighty-six the booze for
you! My luck, wouldn't it be my luck. Vito-baby, you
done it again.

JIMMY. (*Setting up food on plate, cold chicken, cole
slaw, tomato slice etc.*) Your luck! Your luck!!! Who
asked you to drop in, Vito-baby? Not me. Okay, so
pay the consequences, you crumb!

VITO. Don't call me a crumb!

JIMMY. Yeah, or what'll you do? (VITO *is silent.*)
You couldn't tie your shoelaces now. You crumb. You
crummy crumb! You couldn't even pick your nose,

which is something you're undoubtedly extremely adept at.

VITO. (*In honest distaste.*) That's disgusting!

JIMMY. Ahhh! Lord Crumb-bum is offended!

VITO. You know something—you got a mean streak! (JIMMY *has finished plate by here and laughs.*) Very funny. You oughtta see a shrink, you fucked-up excuse for a *soap opera queen!*

JIMMY. (*Rushes to* VITO, *grabs him.*) Listen, punk! You little no-good-petty-goddam-punk-robber. I'll bet you're the same dirty little bastard that robbed me twice before, aren't you?

VITO. No.

JIMMY. Aren't you? (*Shaking him.*) *Aren't you?*

VITO. Let up! Jesus, I was never here before. My mother's word of honor!

JIMMY. Your mother? Your mother's probably a cheap hooker! Where's your mother tonight, you crummy little alley cat, out hooking for New Year's?

VITO. My mother's dead!

JIMMY. Oh, *hooked* herself to death! (*Going to kitchen, getting stand-up tray.*)

VITO. Oh boy—I may be dumb and—but you—you know what you are? You're *perverse!*

JIMMY. (*Placing stand-up tray* D. S. R. *corner of* VITO. *Brooklynese.*) Per-*voice!* Oh—we've been sneaking into the *dictionary*, haven't we? (*Getting chair from desk.*)

VITO. You— I'm not gonna talk to you no more.

JIMMY. Ah . . . ! Don't tell me that. (*Gets flower from table for vase.*) Break my heart, would you? And on New Year's? He's not going to *talk* to me. Farewell, world; so long, Mommy! (*Sits and puts napkin on lap.*) But, just remember, if you change your mind and decide to break your vow of silence— you have to say, "May I?"

VITO. Nut!

JIMMY. Ah-ah, you forgot to say "May I?" (*Light-*

ing candle.) Oh, thanks for the champagne—the $27.00 I found in your pocket bought it. (*Begins to eat.*)

VITO. You're a goddam pickpocket. (*Blows out candle.*)

JIMMY. (*Freezes, mouth open, food inches away, then holds forkful of food toward* VITO; VITO *tries to eat from fork, but* JIMMY *quickly puts food in own mouth.*) Mmm-mmm good!

VITO. You know what I wish? I wish I could puke right now! I'd just love to snap my cookies right in front of you.

JIMMY. (*Slightly nauseated.*) Maybe you should take a course. They offer courses in almost everything nowadays. You could enroll in Puking I, then, if you do well—go on to Puking II. You might even take your *Master's*.

VITO. Whack—oh! Boy, what I wouldn't give for a shot at you! I'd fuckin' total you.

JIMMY. Make up your mind, do you want to *puke,* or do you want to total me? (*Relights candle.*) That's the trouble with you young people today—can't make up your minds. And remember: the decision you make today might affect your entire life. (*Resumes eating.*)

VITO. I think you're flippin'.

JIMMY. And aren't you lucky to be on hand?

VITO. Yeah, my luck! I never saw nothin' like you for mean. Eatin' in front of a person. I didn't eat since last night. I'm goddam hungry! (*Blows out candle.*) If you treated your cat the way you treat people, it's probably a good thing he croaked. Ha!—Ha! Come on, I'm hungry!

JIMMY. Really?

VITO. Yeah, what do you think?

JIMMY. Well, let's see if we can't find something for you. (*Rises, gives* VITO'S *hair an affectionate muss with one hand on his way to refrigerator.*)

VITO. You kiddin'?

JIMMY. (*Taking a small bowl and jar of mayonnaise from refrigerator.*) Would I kid you? We can scrounge up a little something. After all—got to keep you alive for the operation! (*Walking to counter with bowl and mayonnaise jar.*) Besides, I always feed the burglars, that's why they keep coming *back*. (*Adds mayonnaise.*) Here we go, a little mayonnaise, a dash of salt and pepper—you like garlic? (*Liberally sprinkling.*)

VITO. You kiddin'? It's our national flower.

JIMMY. Good. (*Walking toward* VITO.) There, I think you'll be amused by its lack of pretension. (*Putting bowl down on folding table; places folding table* U. C.; *then takes up bowl and spoon.*)

VITO. Huh?

JIMMY. (*Giving him a taste from a spoon.*) There— that okay? (*Sitting.*)

VITO. Damned right it is, I'm hungry! Hey, you gonna feed me the whole thing—like a little baby?

JIMMY. If that's what you'd like. Mangia, Mangia!

VITO. Hey, gratzi, gratzi. (JIMMY *gives him another taste.*) Man, that's good, what is it?

JIMMY. (*Rising, walking to refrigerator, taking out can of cat food.*) Well, let's see . . . Kontented Kitty—

VITO. Oh, Jesus! (*Spitting it out.*) Achh!

JIMMY. (*Walking back to* VITO.) Kontented spelled with a K, that's cute, isn't it? "Guaranteed to give Kitty's coat a high sheen and make Kitty purr." (*Glancing at* VITO.) Your hair looks better already. Can't quite make out the purr yet, but . . . (*Replacing cat food can plus mayonnaise in refrigerator.*)

VITO. You crazy-ass bastard! Jesus, you— (*Blurting it out.*) I'm glad I robbed you before. I'm fuckin' glad I did! Jesus, am I ever!

JIMMY. (*After a beat.*) So you did, didn't you!

VITO. Twice, ripped you off twice, scraped you clean. And I'd do it again. You miserable excuse for a human person!

JIMMY. (*Rushing to* VITO, *grabbing him.*) My book
. . . all those pages. *What did you do with them!*

VITO. *Threw 'em out.* I thought there'd be some
goodies in that box, nothin' but a lot of yellow pages
with—

JIMMY. (*Hitting* VITO.) Bastard! You cretin bastard! (*Kicking the chair Upstage.*) Uck! Look at you.
You don't have to puke to ruin my appetite; just *the
sight of you* is enough!

VITO. Tough shit—you turd!

JIMMY. (*Shouting.*) I've had enough of you! None
of your smart-ass, no lip! Do you hear me?

VITO. Yeah . . .

JIMMY. Yes, sir! Let's hear it!

VITO. (*Small voice.*) Yes, sir.

JIMMY. (*Grabbing* VITO *by the back of the neck.*)
Loud and clear. It's New Year's Eve! Yes, sir!

VITO. (*Normal voice.*) Yes, sir.

JIMMY. Ring it out. Let it echo— *Yes, sir!*

VITO. Yes, sir! (*Then, voice shaky.*) Jesus!

JIMMY. No swearing! The scroungy-petty-little-half-
assed-junkie-burglars don't swear! Have you got that
straight?

VITO. (*Badly rattled.*) Listen, I'll make you a deal.
You tell me what—you know, the worth of everything.
I'll get the money and pay you back.

JIMMY. My *book!* Jesus, how could you—my book
you can't replace.

VITO. You don't got a copy?

JIMMY. *No, I don't got a copy!* Okay, so—so I just
tell you the value of everything else, and—

VITO. —I'll get the money and pay you back.

JIMMY. How? Where would you get the money?

VITO. Some I got, I got some.

JIMMY. Bully. Where do you keep it? Under a rock
over in the East Village? Nothing as common as a
bank, I take it?

VITO. (*Forced into bravado.*) Sure, in a bank. Where else?

JIMMY. Where else indeed? Savings or checking?

VITO. Huh?

JIMMY. Savings or checking account? Do you keep it in a savings or checking account? Or both?

VITO. Yeah, both. Some in each.

JIMMY. Ah, big Diamond Vito Antonucci. Two bank accounts—what bank?

VITO. My bank.

JIMMY. The Vito Antonucci Federal Loan and Trust Company?

VITO. No, come on, the bank I go to.

JIMMY. But what's the name of this bank?

VITO. The—ah, the—

JIMMY. (*Smacking his hands together impatiently.*) Spit it out, man. Come on, come on! (VITO *stutters, trying to find an appropriate "line."*) Hey, maybe this whole thing would go better if you spoke Italian? Is it a language problem, Vito-baby? How do you get your goddam money in and out if you don't know the *name?*

VITO. I do . . . but you yell and . . . Honest, you gotta believe me, I got—

JIMMY. *You got nothing!* On top of everything else, you lied to me, didn't you?

VITO. No! No! I didn't lie!

JIMMY. (*Banging his fists on sink.*) Yes, you did! You lied! You lied! Admit it!

VITO. Yes, yes—okay, lay off. I lied.

JIMMY. Why? *Why?*

VITO. (*Shouting back, close to tears.*) Because—to get outta here. Because—for the main reason—you got me spooked. Looks like you got some, like some big hassles and maybe you're not in such a good mood. And I don't know what you got in your head like *to do* with me.

JIMMY. Good! Good! I'll let you in on something,

the way I feel tonight—I spook myself! (*Laughs.*) I
really do. (*Walking* u. s. *toward bed.*) Great, I never
spooked anyone in my whole life, maybe my luck's
changing. (*Flops down on bed, kicks his feet up in the
air, bicycle-style.*)

VITO. Your luck may be changing, but—somethin'
tells me *my moon* is still in hell. Hey, guy—how come
you didn't just call the cops?

JIMMY. The cops! (*Sits up on bed.*) Oh, yeah, I
called those clowns the first two times you ripped me
off. They were a great help. (*Rises.*) Oh, boy! (*Puts
chair back at desk.*)

VITO. (*Laughing.*) You found out about the knuckle-
heads, did you?

JIMMY. First time—it took the guy five hours to get
here. So excited he fell asleep right over there while
he was making out his report. I had to make him a
pot of coffee so he could finish it. (*Walking toward
the bathroom door.*) Second time, you came through
the small skylight over the bathroom . . .

VITO. Yeah, right—it pried open easier than this one.

JIMMY. (*Walking back* c.) Good—we try to please
. . . *here at Invasion House.* Next time, two clowns
showed up. Asked . . . (*In Brooklynese.*) "How the
poi-petrator affected entry—"

VITO. Yeah, they talk funny.

JIMMY. *They* talk funny? Yeah, you should know.
I took 'em to the john, showed 'em where you shinnied
down . . .

VITO. Yeah, that was a tight squeeze, I remember.

JIMMY. Tight squeeze!? Oh, sorry, next time I'll
grease the walls! *Tight squeeze?* You must have
crawled through a field of mud on your way over here,
from the look of the walls. They were a *cartoon* of
prints. One cop turned to the other and said, "Hey,
look at the crazy wallpaper design. We could call it
Basic Burglar." (VITO *laughs.*) So—go call the cops.

VITO. (*After a long pause.*) Yeah, well, if you ain't gonna call 'em, what *are* you gonna do?

JIMMY. I don't know . . . I don't know. I'm working on it. (*Sits on chaise.*)

VITO. Yeah, well—in the meantime . . . I gotta piss. Would you let me up, just to piss? (*Slight groan.*)

JIMMY. What do you think?

VITO. Honest, I'm telling you, I *gotta* take a leak.

JIMMY. Go ahead.

VITO. Hey, come on, guy!

JIMMY. No, I don't have to. You start without me. Go ahead.

VITO. Hah-hah, very funny. Honest-to-God, my teeth are startin' to float.

JIMMY. Like I said, leak away. You're right over the sink.

VITO. In the *sink!* That's dirty!

JIMMY. It's *my* sink! What do you care?

VITO. Yeah, and they're *my* clothes. Not in my clothes. (JIMMY *chuckles;* VITO *smiles slyly; glances away, then looks back to* JIMMY.) Okay, at least give me a hand . . .

JIMMY. Give you a . . . (*Rises.*) *Give you a hand!*

VITO. Yeah, what's the matter, is it a language problem, Jimmy-baby? Or—you afraid you might like it?

JIMMY. Hey, wait a minute, wait a minute—don't tell me you're *queer!?*

VITO. (*Cocky now, in his own sexual territory.*) What are you—takin' a census?

JIMMY. No, I don't believe it; I don't believe it! I finally catch the punk that's robbed me twice, tie him up and he turns out to be queer? What is it with me? Not after everything else today! (*Looking up.*) Hey, *you up there*—you didn't even have time to *reload!* (*Back to* VITO.) You're not—no, you're not actually *queer*, are you?

VITO. (*Casually.*) Tell you what—why don't you unzip me and take it out. If it starts to grow, you got your answer! Then if *yours* starts to grow, I got myself . . .

JIMMY. (*Rushing to* VITO, *threatening to slap him.*) You cretin! You cretin!

VITO. (*Ducking as much as he can.*) Oh-ho, what'd I—hit a nerve? Got a little *problem?* And tell me you don't swing both ways! I never met an actor yet didn't swing. (*Sudden harsh laugh.*) Listen, go ahead—do me a favor? Call the cops. Hand me the phone, *I'll* call 'em. It's New Year's Eve, plus I didn't take nothin'. What are they gonna do?

JIMMY. You didn't take nothin'? You robbed me twice before, you admitted it.

VITO. You really are some kind of yo-yo. What?— you got that on tape? You think I'd cough that up to the Keystones? Your word against mine; you got no evidence. *Hah, I'm just gettin' a big flash.* You said you spooked yourself; I just figured out why. See, you got yourself in what they call a—like a— dichotomy. How's that for sneakin' into the old Webster? I'll translate: you ain't got a clue about what to do with me. You got a Mexican stand-off on your hands. So—come on, goddamit, let me up! I gotta piss, and I'm too old to start wettin' my goddam pants!

JIMMY. And I'm too old to start taking orders from punks.

VITO. We got this problem, could get *very messy.* So—what are you gonna do?

JIMMY. Don't rush me. I—I've got to put on my thinkin' cap.

VITO. *Your thinking cap!* I think you lost that at the cleaners. For the main reason—I heard this rumor you flunked Imagination I *AND* Imagination II. Yeah, I heard somewhere—I forget exactly—you didn't have a fresh idea in your head how to present yourself. Everything by the rules, you let everyone dump all over your head, you don't got a clue about what to do with me!

JIMMY. Hey, remember *me?* None of your lip, none of your cracks, no more smart-ass! You're not the boss around here, you're just a—a—little piece of immobile shit! (*Walking into the kitchen, looking for something.*) So you really have to pee, huh?

VITO. Yeah, how many times do I gotta tell you!

JIMMY. Well, let's see if we can't come up with a solution, man being the inventive genius he is. (*Going to the desk, rummaging through the drawers.*)

VITO. How do you mean?

JIMMY. (*Locating a pair of scissors, holding them behind his back.*) Ah—here we go. (*Moving toward VITO's feet.*) I'll show you a little "imagination."

VITO. Whatcha gonna do?

JIMMY. Let it be a surprise! (*Snips scissors.*)

VITO. (*Cranes his neck around as JIMMY holds up the cuff of his S. R. pants leg and cuts.*) Jesus—no—hey, my pants! Hey, I don't have to go! Honest, I don't! *Truth.* I made it up. I just said that to—get off of here.

JIMMY. (*Cutting from the cuff up the center of the back of one leg.*) Little boys who cry wolf—end up getting their pants cut off.

VITO. (*Yelling.*) You nut! You bug-brained crazy-ass nut!

JIMMY. Careful—especially during surgery!

VITO. Come on, that ain't funny! My pants! How am I supposed to get home?

JIMMY. (*Cutting up backs of one trouser leg, then the other.*) Who said anything about going home? Some people have a pet dog, some have a pet cat. My cat's dead; so I got a pet *Vito.* (*Carrying on imaginary conversation, going into Vitoese.*) Oh, you got a pet *Vito?* They're rare, aren't they? Rare! You can't hardly get them no more. Where'd you get your Vito—at the Vito store? No, by God, I found

mine right under the bed. Under the *bed?* Yes, Vitos
are a lot like cats that way, they adopt you, you don't
adopt them. What about housebreaking? Oh, no problem at all, matter of fact, I'm training mine to go in
the *kitchen sink!*

VITO. You are really playin' with half a deck!

JIMMY. Hey, what nifty little shorts! Paisley, very
natty! (*Begins cutting through shorts.*)

VITO. Those ain't shorts—I got my ass tattooed!
My pants—you wrecked my pants. Mean! Boy, I
pulled some bummers in my life, but at least I ain't
mean like you!

JIMMY. I'd say your frame of reference is somewhat
removed from life as we know it on this planet.

VITO. Get the big Pants Cutter—no shit!

JIMMY. No shit! One more snip and you're free as a
bird. (*Finishes the cutting, grabs hold of the pants
and shorts.*) Lift up!

VITO. Lift up yourself.

JIMMY. (*Pokes* VITO *with scissors point.*) Lift up.
(VITO *lifts up and* JIMMY *pulls trousers and under-
wear out from under* VITO, *rushes to window, drops
clothes out and down.*) Wheeeeee! (*Then, turns back
to* VITO, *focuses for the first time on his bare behind,
realizes what he's done, turns away nervously, a combination of elation, remorse, confusion.*)

VITO. (*After a long beat, glances around.*) How do
you like the act so far? Nice smile, no teeth, huh?
(*Looking around at his bare behind.*) That's funny,
I feel a draft! Hey, you like fruit? Take a bite of
my ass—it's a peach!

JIMMY. Shut up and pee!

VITO. I told you, I don't *have to!*

JIMMY. Fake it!

VITO. (*Sarcastic put-on.*) You're very—vivid! Boy,
are you ever. You're a very vivid person. (*Suddenly
bursts into laughter.*) Oh . . . Oh, mother . . .

JIMMY. What's so funny?

VITO. Oh—oh, now you really done it. We got a whole new ballgame. *Now* you can't call the cops! How are you gonna explain the bare-ass bit? "Dah . . . dah, officer, officer . . . I caught this burglar and I . . . dah . . . dah, well, you see, I—ah—his pants just sort of self-destructed themselves." (*TELE-PHONE RINGS.*) I can see it in the papers: ACTOR MOLESTS BURGLAR IN GREENWICH VIL-LAGE.

JIMMY. (*Answering the phone.*) Hello . . . Oh, hi, Janie . . . Yeah, fired . . . Well, it hit kinda hard at first, but . . .

VITO. (*Shouting.*) Help, I'm being took advantage of! The big actor, Freddie Footlights, is mo*lest*ing me!

JIMMY. (*Speaking into phone.*) No, I'm not alone. Lee Strasberg dropped by; we're improvising . . . Costume party? . . . I don't feel much like a costume party tonight . . . Sure, I get a kick out of Carmine, but I really don't—

VITO. (*Shouting.*) Help! Call out the Vice Squad, this weird-do has me all naked and . . . (JIMMY *holds out the receiver to* VITO *as he did earlier.*)

VITO. Aw, nuts . . .

JIMMY. Oh, ah—listen, Janie, when Carmine gets there—ah, have him call me. Tell him I got a—ah—no, no forget it, I was only . . .

VITO. (*Mimicking* JIMMY.) Dah—dah, I got this—ah . . . I dunno . . . (*Makes Bronx-cheer/raspberry sound.*)

JIMMY. No, Janie, wait! Yeah, do have Carmine call. *Tell him I have something for him* . . . Oh, just a little something in the way of a warm body.

VITO. Big deal.

JIMMY. I mean it . . . I can't help it if it doesn't sound like me . . . Specialty? Don't worry about Carmine's *specialty.* This creature will go for any-thing . . . Just have Carmine call me. 'Bye. (*Hangs*

up, laughs.) Oh, Vito, have I got something for *you!*
Crazy Carmine.

VITO. Crazy Carmine, huh? This specialty—what's
his specialty?

JIMMY. Uh . . . Just a little thing he does with—
figs and mice. (*Picks up folding table and carries it to
kitchen.*)

VITO. Figs and *mice?*

JIMMY. Yeah, what's the matter, you don't like
mice?

VITO. No, it's the figs that bug me. (*Snickering.*)
Figs and mice. So . . . what are you gonna do—
watch? What's a' matter? You gotta call somebody
else in to do a man's job? You can't do your own work?

JIMMY. I wouldn't touch you with a ten-foot pole.
(*Walks to bed, straightening it up.*)

VITO. So—get a twelve-foot pole! Hey, you know
how to break a Pole's finger? Hit him in the nose.

JIMMY. Very funny. You ought to have your own
pizza stand.

VITO. Yeah, but while I'm waitin' for the bank
loan, I know it's dumb to ask—but could I have a
cigarette? There's a pack of cigarettes right over there.

JIMMY. I know where they are, I live here! (*Walks
to table, getting the cigarettes.*) I guess you can have
one.

VITO. I could?

JIMMY. Sure, what the hell—it's New Year's Eve—
live it up! (*An imitation of Karloff.*) Who knowth—
it may be your lahstht! (*Gutteral laugh as he crosses
to* VITO.) Ba-ha-ha-ha-ah!

VITO. Whackerooney!

JIMMY. Here. (*Lights cigarette for him.*)

VITO. (*He takes a puff;* JIMMY *removes the cigarette.*) Thanks. Take one. (JIMMY *walks to table and
drops lighter.*)

JIMMY. I gave it up. (*Returns to* VITO; JIMMY *still
holding lit cigarette.*)

VITO. Oh, Jack Armstrong! The All-American Boy! Oh, that's the greatest! (*Breaks up with laughter.*)

JIMMY. What's so funny now?

VITO. (*Taking another drag.*) Kills me. He beats people up, knocks them-the-fuck-out, ties them up, cuts their clothes off—but he don't *smoke*. Oh, no, nothin' like that!

KATE. (*Offstage.*) Jimmy . . . (*Onstage.*) Jimmy . . . ? (KATE *stops on landing.*)

JIMMY. (*Standing by* VITO, *he quickly decides to play the Scene with equanimity and "put on"* KATE.) Oh, hi. Come on in.

VITO. Yeah, join the fun!

JIMMY. (*Going to her, takes her hand, leads her into room; she tends to pull back.*) Yeah, what the hell, the more the merrier. Come on in. What a surprise?

KATE. (*Goggle-eyed.*) Surprise!

JIMMY. Yes. I had no idea you'd be dropping by. Did you, Vito?

VITO. No, she didn't say nothin' to me. (KATE *walks farther into the room, eyes glued to the sight of* VITO.)

JIMMY. (*To* KATE.) Where's your date? Thought you were off for a smashing New Year's? (*She is too stunned to speak;* JIMMY *crowds her toward sink.*) Kate, where's your date? I thought you were off for parties and skiing and laughing and scratching. (*She continues to stare.*) Kate?

KATE. We, ah—were. I mean, we are, but—

JIMMY. Where's your escort? (*Snaps his fingers for her attention.*) Kate, where's your date?

KATE. Down . . . ah, down . . . in the car. When I—ah, when— (*Circling the sink unit, alternately glancing at* VITO *and avoiding looking at him.*) I—ah, called up I got—I just—I mean, I could hear *yelling* and I got worried.

VITO. If he was doing the things to you he does to me—you'd yell, too. (JIMMY *puts out cigarette.*)

KATE. Jimmy? What is this? You said—a burglar?

JIMMY. Well, a burglar-friend. Burglar-buddy. (*Walking to* D. S. R. *sink corner.*) That's it, a combination burglar-type-friend-buddy-*pal*. (*Leaning up against sink, near* VITO's *head.*)

KATE. But naked . . . ?

JIMMY. Well, ah, you know . . .

VITO. (*Rubbing his head against* JIMMY's *chest.*) That's where the buddy part comes in. (KATE *turns away.*)

JIMMY. Yeah. Say, why don't you ask your friend up for a glass of milk and a cookie, huh? No hard feelings.

VITO. Yeah, ask him up. Maybe we can, you know—all have a little party?

KATE. No. No, I don't think—

VITO. Come on, it's New Year's! Is he humpy? (JIMMY *laughs.*)

KATE. *What?*

VITO. Is he *humpy!?*

JIMMY. Yeah, what's his name? (*Going to* U. S. *window.*) I'll call down to him. (*Opens window and whistles out it.*)

KATE. (*Hurrying to* JIMMY, *pulling him back* D. S.) No, Jimmy—don't! He wouldn't—no, please, don't! No, no!

JIMMY. We wouldn't want to do anything to dampen the romance.

KATE. Jimmy?

JIMMY. Yes.

KATE. Did you *stage* this? Huh, did you?

JIMMY. *Stage* it?

KATE. Yes, come on, what's going on? I don't get it.

VITO. (*Playing it very straight.*) What—didn't you know he swung both ways?

KATE. (*Flustered.*) I—ah, I wasn't talking to you!

VITO. But I'm talkin' to *you*, Angel-Bumps. Or did you think you was the only one gettin' in on those great *hugglebunnyburgers!* (JIMMY *goes to the chaise, sits.*) We call ours *Bangaramathons.* But what's the diff? Hugglebunnyburgers—Bangaramathons, six of one—

VITO and JIMMY. —half a dozen of the other!

VITO. What ya' lose on the peanuts, ya' make up on the bananas—right?

KATE. (*Incredulous.*) *Jimmy!* What's the—

VITO. We been makin' it since last August 22nd on and off; I mean he really knows how to toss the old salad. So tonight—

KATE. Well, I—Jimmy!

FRED'S VOICE. (*Offstage.*) Kate . . . you okay?

KATE. (*Sinks down on hassock* C.) Oh, Christ—

FRED'S VOICE. You said you'd only be a minute—

(FRED GABLE, *good-looking, thirty-fivish, well-turned-out, enters, half-looking behind him.*)

FRED. —What is this? No lights in the hall, no one else living here, I tell you, this building's really . . . (*Catches sight of* VITO.) It's—uh—a very unusual apartment. Well, ah, I guess you'd call it one of those loft-type, Greenwich Village-type apartments. (JIMMY *walks to* S. L. *at sink.*)

KATE. (*Rises, crosses to* FRED.) Oh, Fred, I was just coming down. Ah—Jimmy, this is Fred Gable. Fred—Jimmy Zoole. (JIMMY *extends his hand across* VITO'S *behind.*)

FRED. (*Moves to* S. R. *of sink; tentatively at first, then thrusts hand across* VITO'S *behind to shake.*) How's it goin'?

JIMMY. Very interesting! Fred, I'd like you to meet Vito, Vito Antonucci. He can't shake hands right now—he's tied up.

FRED. Isn't that funny, but I caught *that.* Almost right off, I—ah, figured that one out. I was always quick, even in school. Yeah, not only that, I also noticed he doesn't have any *pants* on.

VITO. (*To* FRED.) Humpy. (*To* KATE.) Hum-pee!

FRED. What was that?

VITO. Humpy.

FRED. That's what I thought you said. Well, so far so good. I—ah, passed the sight test *and* the hearing test. Okay . . .

VITO. How's it hangin', Freddie—loose?

KATE. (*Going to* FRED, *taking his arm.*) Well, ah— we'd better be running along. I just stopped by to—

VITO. (*Quickly.*) Oh, come on. Stick around, we'll plug an onion!

KATE. (*Giggling nervously.*) Well . .

VITO. Or we could have a taffy pull! You pull mine, I'll pull yours. (KATE *giggles again.*)

FRED. (*To* KATE.) You think that's funny?

KATE. (*Indicating* VITO.) What—*that?*

FRED. No, stick around, plug an onion, or the taffy pull—or *that?* Yeah . . . what the heck, while we're at it—I'll go for the big one. What is *that?*

KATE. Well . . .

JIMMY. Oh, I thought I introduced you. Vito Antonucci, Fred—ah—Garble.

FRED. *Gable.* And your last name's— *Zoole?* Garble . . . that's cute.

KATE. (*Lightly, giggling.*) Gable-Garble, Tomato-tom-ahto.

FRED. (*Walking to* KATE.) Oh . . . that's cute, too. That's real cute.

KATE. Well . . . (*Another sigh.*)

FRED. You know, that's the third time you've sighed and said, "Well . . ."

KATE. Really? (*Shrugs, sighs.*) Well—oh, Christ, I did it again! I mean, well, it's New Year's, I guess I can sigh and say "Well" if I want to. (*Sits on chaise.*)

FRED. Okay, let's level—huh? I've got a sense of humor same as the next guy.

VITO. You ain't racked up any weepers so far.

FRED. (*To* JIMMY, *ignoring* VITO.) Is this—is this

what they call Off-off-off Broadway? And are there
performances every night, or is this the . . . ah,
special New Year's Eve *Whoopee* Show? *Or is it some*
crazy new way to unplug a sink? (JIMMY *awards*
FRED *points for this, mutters "Ah-hah," gives him the*
high-sign, FRED *acknowledges this, takes a little bow.*)

KATE. Oh, Fred, can't you take a joke?

JIMMY. (*Walking to dart board on wall near bed.*)
Oh, didn't Kate tell you about our little games? (*Tak-*
ing a handful of darts.) Kate, how could you be so
negligent? (*Going to* FRED.) Now—no fair throwing
them straight at him, though. You gotta lob 'em up
in the air, like this. (*Offering* FRED *the darts.*) Wanna
try a few? (FRED *demurs.*)

VITO. Yeah, hit my ass and win a Cadillac!

FRED. Okay, Kate. Did I flunk the test? I give up—
wanna let me in on the gig? (JIMMY *begins to play*
darts.) Come on, you know the guy, what's going on?

KATE. Frankly, I haven't a clue. I don't know.

JIMMY. That's the first time in seventeen months
I ever heard you admit you don't know something.
(*To* FRED, *laughing.*) Oh, Freddy, are you in for it!

FRED. It's a regular laugh-riot around here! (*To*
KATE.) Sweet and sorta *square,* you said. (KATE *rises.*)
If this is your idea of square, we're in for one helluva
weekend. (FRED *walks toward the front door.*) Come
on, Kate. (*On top of step.*) Oh, uh, gentlemen, good
luck—whatever it is you do! (*Exits.*)

KATE. (*To* JIMMY.) I'll get you for this! (*To* VITO.)
And you, *whoever* you are—I hope he scores a bull's-
eye! (*She exits.*)

VITO. So do I, Angel-Tits! (JIMMY *follows her to*
door, closes it, and walks back to C.) Blew her mind!

JIMMY. (*Both he and* VITO *are laughing.*) Banga-
ramathon!

VITO. We really blew her stack!

JIMMY. —And August 22nd! Where'd you pull that
from? (*Flops on chaise.*)

Vito. August 22nd? That's my birthday, I'm Leo. See, I used to be a chronic liar and—

Jimmy. *Used to be?*

Vito. I learned—if you hit people with the specifics of the issue, they swallow it. (*Jumping the gun.*) Okay, come on, get these ropes off me; this position is a bitch! (Jimmy *only looks at him.*) Come on, Jimmy-baby, chop-chop. The show's over. I did my schtick; we put the zilch on Angel-Tits, now let me the fuck up!

Jimmy. Hey, wait a minute, wait a minute—

Vito. I get to get up now!

Jimmy. No comprendo?

Vito. Come on, you gotta! *Now, you gotta!*

Jimmy. No, I don't, I don't *gotta* do nothin', for nobody! (*Rises.*)

Vito. No . . . ?

Jimmy. Not on your life!

Vito. But *why?* . . . Jesus!

Jimmy. Number one, Vito-baby, you jumped the gun. Bad timing! You think because we put one over on Angel-Tits, that settles the score? Well, let me tell you something— (*Walking toward* Vito.)

Vito. First, I'll tell *you* something! You're an A-Number-One-Prick! Yeah, an' without the catsup!

Jimmy. Listen, you ignorant-little-wop-bastard, I worked for ten months of grinding, brain-bending work—and you come along and throw it out with the *trash!*

Vito. You wrote it once, you could write it again, couldn't you?

Jimmy. (*Pacing.*) I can't just sit here on a velvet cushion writing while the servants fix dinner. I have to look for work.

Vito. What about this rich aunt of yours? This— ah, Claire?

Jimmy. So, what are *you* all of a sudden, a social worker?

VITO. I'm just trying to help.

JIMMY. You! I've had enough help from *you!*

VITO. Okay! You know what ga-noog is? It's Jewish. It means enough, like enough is enough! Comes a time when you've had your kicks with me and then, baby, ga-noog is ga-noog.

JIMMY. No threats from you—crumb! A crumb doesn't make threats.

VITO. That's another thing. You can call me a lot of things—but crumb isn't one of them! You can do a lot of things to a person, but when you mortify a person, a person don't forget! And just remember, Jimmy-baby, you gotta let me up sometime and then— watch out! 'Cause when it comes to gettin' even, I'm sly as a shit-house rat!

JIMMY. (*Through gritted teeth.*) Don't threaten me —you crumb!

VITO. (*Screaming.*) *Ga-noog, you bastard!*

JIMMY. (*Yelling.*) You think you've had ga-noog from me! You little creeps think you can go around this city robbing and mugging and fucking up everything you touch! You haven't had half a ga-noog outta me! Not one more word, not one threat or you're gonna regret it the rest of your crummy life! (*Each word spelled out.*) *Have you got that straight?* (VITO *doesn't reply.*) *Have you?*

VITO. Yes. (JIMMY *walks to hassock and sits.*) Yeah. Jesus, what are you going to do with me?

JIMMY. I don't know, but one thing for sure, Vito-baby— (*Thrusting a finger out at him.*) I'm gonna break my ass . . . to make it "imaginative."

LIGHTS DOWN—MUSIC UP

END OF ACT ONE

ACT TWO

SCENE 1

VITO *is still tied down on sink; he is alone in the room. A BEAT.* JIMMY *enters from* U. S. *bathroom, in different trousers and shirt, with hand-towel over shoulder, carrying champagne glass and after-shave bottle.*

JIMMY. I just had the most interesting experience, Vito. (*Puts glass on top of bench.*)

VITO. So did I—my back is broken.

JIMMY. (*Applies aftershave, puts bottle down, then walks to closet, gets smoking jacket and puts it on, during:*) Oh, we'll take care of that. We will. But let me tell you: There I was, getting ready for New Year's, looking in the mirror, shaving. And I looked at that face staring back at me, and I said: "Hmn, I know that fellow, yes, I do . . . but he looks so different. Wonder what it could be?" Then it all flooded in on me, all the *magnificent* things that have happened today—and I thought, just for a second, there in the mirror: "What's to become of the poor wretch?" But only for a split-second, because then I focused on the eyes and there was a glint in them and, by God, I didn't look all that put-upon, didn't look like life had gotten to be too much for me at all. I simply looked like I'd gone mad, and I suddenly realized— *that's probably what had taken place!* Yes, it was all out of my hands and I thought: "Christ, what a relief! It's all out of my hands." I don't have to deal with things like I did before, or go around being *nice, pleasing* everybody. (*Imaginary conversation.*) Hello! How are you? Nice to see you! Understudy the German Shepherd? Sure, why not. (*Back to* VITO.) No,

50

no more. Because now I'm going to be nice to me! Isn't that interesting? (VITO *only looks at him.*) Oh, that's right, your back was breaking. (*Gets a pillow from the bed.*) We'll take care of that. Because I also got a huge flash about what we're going to do with *you.* Lift up a bit. (*Stuffing pillow under* VITO, S. R. *side.*) There, that better? (*Starts toward chaise, then turns back.*) Ahh! Say, I hope you don't have a "thing" for pillows! Huh? (*Sits on hassock, just* R. *of* VITO.) All right, now this is the schedule. First we're going to have our New Year's—and then, this is what struck me: you broke into my home and destroyed—oh, just about a year's work, a lot of good basic material. Well, now I am intensely interested in the kind of—ah—sociological phenomenon that could do a thing like that. So now *you're* going to provide *me* with some *new* material. You're going to give me an in-depth interview, you're going to spill the beans on what it's like to be—*you*—whatever that is. We're not quite sure. But first—New Year's. (*Goes to kitchen, gets paper party bag, returns and puts party hat on* VITO, *slipping the strap under his chin.*) Wasn't I lucky to find these? I tell you, you can get anything in the Village. (*Tipping the hat to the side.*) There, that's a bit jauntier. But still, you don't look all that festive. Must be something missing. Oh, would you like your horn now? (*Gets it, blows on it;* VITO *ignores him.*) No? All right, I'll put it right here, just in case. (*Checks his watch.*) We have . . . not *even* two minutes to go. *Can you wait?* (*Going to kitchen for champagne, gets saucer, places it on sink in front of* VITO.) I think for New Year's, you can have your own saucer of champagne. That way you won't have to depend upon me, in case I get carried away with the festivities. (*Pours champagne for* VITO.) There you go. Lap it up, there's more where that came from. (VITO *turns his head away.*) I hope you're not going to sulk. Don't sulk! (*Puts down his champ. Walks to desk* U. S. C.) I know how to cheer you up, yes, indeed— (*Gets Instamatic camera from desk drawer, walks* D. S. C. *and focuses camera from* D. S. R. *of sink.*) I don't suppose you'd give us a little smile? (VITO *hides his face in tied hands.* VITO *turns his head to the side, cheek down on the block;* JIMMY *hurries to* D. S. L.) Hmmnn, that's not bad. Sorta sweet, cheek down, in repose. Playing against type. (*He takes the shot.*) Good. (*Walks* U. S. *of* VITO *for rear-view shot.*) Just one more. Don't suppose you'd give us a little smile *now?* (*Takes another photo.*) Say, if that one comes out good, you might even use it for your Christmas card next year. (*Stows camera in desk, gets cassette recorder from atop TV.*) And when we get to the interview, I think we'll just *record* it. (JIMMY *checks cassette recorder out.*) Testing, one, two, three. (*Goes to stool* U. S. *of sink, places stool below sink. Sings:*) "Some enchanted evening, you will meet a stranger. You will meet a stranger—" Mmn, all systems go—look at that needle jump! (*Places cassette on stool near* VITO, *checks his watch again.*) Another thirty seconds, and we got a dead year on our hands. And what a *great* year it's been! (*Gets TV and places it on hassock facing* VITO.) I cannot wait to see what they got lined up for me next. When you think of all the goodies they cook up for us—Jesus must really love his children! (*Smacks his hands together.*) Okay, Vito— Magic Time. (JIMMY *pulls up rabbit ears and turns on TV set, then puts on party hat, gets champagne and toy horn;* VITO *turns to watch for a moment, as:*)

TV ANNOUNCER. (*Voice-over. Shouting.*) We've switched away from the Taft Hotel—here we are in the heart of Times Square, thronged, absolutely jam-packed with curb-to-curb people, despite the heaviest snow in more than three years. (*Sound of an increased crowd roar.*) And there goes the ball of light and the countdown begins: Ten, nine, eight, seven, six, five, four, three, two *and* one— *Happy New Year!* (*There is now an enormous crowd roar: whistles, bells, shouting.* VITO *is crying and buries head in hand.*)

TV BANDLEADER. (*Voice-over. Over "Auld Lang Syne."*) And here we are back at the Taft Hotel. Happy New Year to all of you from all of us—as our happy couples dance in the New Year.

(VITO *is sobbing;* JIMMY *watches him; soon* JIMMY *flicks off the TV set.*)

VITO. (*Crying out.*) Keep it on, keep it on!

JIMMY. (*Grabbing cassette and holding it up to* VITO.) Ladies and gentlemen, the sounds you are now hearing are the actual real live sounds of a burglar crying.— (*A pause.*) That was a sob! Please don't send in donations. Just break out your Kleenex. I think we've got a little three-hankie-number here.

VITO. (*Crying out.*) Jesus, have a heart—can't you?

JIMMY. I—ah, think we'll have to pause slightly while . . . (*Crying is getting to him.*) I hope you're not going to put a damper on our New Year's Eve. Are you? Well, what the hell's the matter with you, anyway?

VITO. (*Snapping his head up.*) What's the matter? Nothin', nothin'— I got a hangnail. What's the *matter?* (*Sniffles.*) Shit, I can't even blow my own nose . . .

JIMMY. (*Goes to kitchen, grabs paper toweling.*) Christ, don't want you blubbering all over the place . . . (*Walks to sink, starts to hold the towel up to* VITO's *nose; then instead, starts untying his hands.*) Here, you can blow your own nose. I've got you strapped down; you can't get up unless you got some Houdini tricks up your sleeve. There. (VITO *blows his nose.*)

VITO. Thanks. (*Throws towel on floor, flexes his hands.*) Great—now I can play the vibra-harp again.

Huh, *what's the matter?* (JIMMY *moves TV to bench
u. s.*) Some comedian. *What's the matter?* I planned
on spending New Year's Eve like this, didn't you
know? Christ, I made my reservations in fucking-
October just to be sure I wouldn't miss it! *What's the
matter?* My whole fucked up life's the matter!

JIMMY. *What the hell do you think I got here—*
a piece of cake? But you don't see me crying about it.
(*Stamps foot.*) No more crying, goddamnit! (*Walking
to* VITO.) All right, let's settle down now. Number
one—

VITO. Number one, I wouldn't tell you the price of
a jelly bean. I wouldn't grant you an interview if—

JIMMY. You'll *grant* me an interview if you want to
get out of here. Remember, I can keep you here as
long as I want. I have no work to go to, no appoint-
ments, nothing to do but—*burglar-sit.* The maid
doesn't come for another five days and when she does
—she can just dust around you. It's your choice, make
up your mind.

VITO. You mean, you'd let me up . . . if I talk.

JIMMY. If you talk straight, don't try to con me.
I want to hear the Gospel According to St. Vito.

VITO. —You gotta deal. Go.

JIMMY. Okay, we got a deal. (*Turns on cassette,
kneels on hassock.*) Now tell me, you break into another man's home, his own private place; twice you
rip him off, clean him out. You *soil* his home, make
it dirty—so he doesn't even like living there anymore . . .

VITO. (*Urgently.*) Whaddya want?

JIMMY. (*Nose to nose.*) When you do something
like that—how does that make you feel?

VITO. (*Looking right at* JIMMY.) Makes me feel
like a crumb. Yeah, like a dirty-little-petty-goddamn-
robbing-bastard. Like a punk—yeah, a crumb . . .

JIMMY. (*Walking away from him, taken off-guard.*)
—I—ah—oh—hmn . . . well . . .

VITO. Heavy question, heavy answer! Hey, I'd loosen up a lot more if I had a little smoke; then I'd really talk. It's like truth serum. The stuff's right in a little plastic sack in my airline bag under your bed.

JIMMY. *Marijuana?* I don't want some whacked-out zombie on my hands.

VITO. No, no . . . just opens me up. Come on, god-dammit, you got a depressed person *on your hands,* and that don't make for good talk.

JIMMY. (*Yelling.*) *Depressed* person? What do you think this is—Pat Boone! (*Note: or "Peter Pan" in areas where he's not known.*)

VITO. Well, we oughtta be able to come up with somethin'—if we ain't gonna smoke. Hey, I got it, why don't we just—make it?

JIMMY. (*Unbelieving.*) *Make it?*

VITO. Yeah, you're here and I sure-in-the-fuck-am. Besides, you're humpy, in an off-beat sort of way.

JIMMY. You're calling *me* off-beat?

VITO. Yeah, you got this . . . something, like they just took the bandages off.

JIMMY. I don't believe tonight; I don't believe what they hit me with! Look, just *eighty-six* the make-out talk. (*Pause.*) Hey—if you were being straight with me, and ripping people off makes you feel that rotten, why don't you get into another line of work?

VITO. I been all fouled up lately, account of per-sonal tragedy which I had in my life. Tonight I needed bread to buy some presents for my daughter; I didn't get to see her over Christmas and—

JIMMY. Your *daughter?* But—what was that big pitch just now?

VITO. Listen, guy—queer, not queer, who's countin'; that's old-fashioned. (*Idea hits.*) That's right, I forgot, you're thirty-eight; you belong to that in-between-generation, the un-hip one. Yeah, you came in right at the ass-end of it, didn't you? Are you queer?

JIMMY. No.

VITO. Ever been married?

JIMMY. No.

VITO. (*Sly.*) Mmn . . . And thirty-eight too—uh-huh?

JIMMY. Hey, stop the presses!—*who's* interviewing *who* here?

VITO. Yeah, right, right. Anyhow, *I* been married, married at sixteen, got a daughter nine, so don't give me that oh-my-shocked-ass-you're-queer bit. Double-gaited, okay; versatile, *definitely*.

JIMMY. And you have a daughter nine?

VITO. Yeah, Melody Antonucci. Ain't *that* a pisser to hang on a kid? Not my idea; my wife's. But gettin' back to Topic A: Ben said "queer" was a word like tall; everybody's a little tall, even a midget; (*Gestures between thumb and forefinger.*) It's *how* tall.

JIMMY. Hold on. You think that's Topic A? Wrong. That's not the topic under discussion tonight, what we do with our genitals. That may be your big concern, but it's not mine. Have you got that straight?

VITO. Okay, cool by me. Then get these straps off me, and let me-the-fuck-up! (*Reaches back, tugs at rope around his back.*)

JIMMY. *We're not finished.*

VITO. All right, like I said before: Give me my smoke. No smokee, no talkee.

JIMMY. (*Going to airline bag, D. S. L. end of bed, as* VITO *drinks champagne from saucer in front of him.*) Okay, smoke your lungs out, see if I care. But talk! . . . (*Goes to* VITO, *hands him the baggie.*) Who's this Ben?

VITO. (*Foraging in the plastic bag for a joint.*) "My Friend." He "bought the farm." That's the personal tragedy I referred to. He's with Jimmy Hoffa now. Only good thing that ever happened to me, and then . . . Ben, he had a peek at the original blueprints; he seen the elephant and heard the hooty owl. He was something else! Hey, how about a little *Fuego* here?

JIMMY. *Fuego?*

VITO. Fire, fire—Jesus! (JIMMY *walks to table, gets lighter, returns and lights end of joint.*) Now the wife, *she* was somethin' else, too. Marcy. Ex, she's remarried. (*Takes "toke," speaks while holding it down for a while.*) Met when we was—she was fourteen, I was fifteen. I thought she hung the moon. Talk about tender, and talk about hugglebunnyburgers! We made 'em like they was gonna burn the recipe! On the roof, in the basement, on the fire escape, the balcony at Loew's 86th Street, right in the middle of Park Avenue, you know that place in the center, with the tulips and the cars whizzin' by? *Unbelievable!* (*Holds joint out.*) Wanna hit?

JIMMY. (*Gets ashtray, brings it to* VITO.) Nah, nah it doesn't work for me.

VITO. Oh, one of *those.* You give me a kick. (JIMMY *walks back to chaise.*) But then she got pregnant with Melody, and after her old man and three brothers took turns beating me up—bein' as how everybody *loved* everybody else—we got married. See Catholics, the Old Country Wop-and-Mick-kind, Christ, if a gorilla banged their daughter and they could *catch* him—zap, get 'em to the church on time! (*Doing imitation.*) "But, Daddy, I don't wanna marry no gorilla!" "Shut up and put on your vail; you fucked a gorilla, you gonna marry a gorilla!" Then, after the baby come, all of a sudden Marcy turned bitter; she got lockjaw-of-the-legs. Me out on the sofa, her and Melody in the bedroom. She'd only let me sleep with her like a reward. My birthday, or if I painted the kitchen, or . . . and then she'd just lay there like she was putting on a brave show for the dentist! I had to split finally, for the main reason— I couldn't stop loving her. My kid. Oh, what a little tiny baby doll. Like porcelain, she is. She— (*The PHONE RINGS.*) If that's my old lady, don't let her know I'm here; she don't like me to hang out with *actors.*

JIMMY. (*Answering the phone.*) Hello . . . Oh, hi,

Kate . . . Happy New Year! Yes, he's still here . . .
Darling, don't shout. I'm just taking your advice, I'm
getting my life uncapped . . . Kate, I can't go into it
right now . . . Darling, it's just that you caught us at
a—well, at a sort of crucial time. Right, Vito? (*Holds
out the phone.*)

VITO. (*Panting.*) Ah . . . oh . . . ahhh . . . Ohh-
hhhhhhh . . . yeah . . . umm . . . !

JIMMY. See what I mean? 'Bye, 'Bye, Angel, love to
Freddie. (*Hangs up, laughing, breaks the connection,*
leaving the phone off the hook.)

VITO. You are a *pisser,* Jimmy Zoole!

JIMMY. Wow, I hope she doesn't come back; I don't
know what we'd do for an encore.

VITO. I do. (*Pause.*) Hey, if you're shakin' it up,
getting your life uncapped—how come you won't take
a little smoke?

JIMMY. I told you, I've tried it a couple times—
nothing.

VITO. Bat-shit! You'd get a kick outta this; this
stuff's guaranteed to make a chihuahua snap at a bull-
dog's ass. (JIMMY *sits on chaise.*) Oh, I get it, you're
scared.

JIMMY. I'm not scared!

VITO. Sure you are. You're afraid if you got high,
you'd let me up.

JIMMY. Oh, no, I wouldn't.

VITO. Betcha. If I win, you gotta make it with me.

JIMMY. And what if I win?

VITO. Hey, I wouldn't make a one-sided bet, I'd be
a sport. If you win, I gotta make it with *you!* . . .
But you're chicken, I can tell. I think Kate was right
about you. Chicken, chicken, chicken! (*Imitates a
chicken.*) Puck-puck-pa-kaw!

JIMMY. After everything that's gone down today and
tonight—you think I'm scared of you or that dumb
little cigarette. (*Rises, walks to* VITO.) You've got to
be kidding! Here. (*Takes joint from* VITO, *inhales a*

quick puff, exhales and hand it back.) There . . . nothing.

VITO. Guy, you *smoke* like Pat Boone! Here, watch, (*Taking a deep "toke."*) You take it way in, suck it down . . . (*Talking while holding the smoke down.*) An' you hold it down with all you got, just like you was holdin' back a fart in an elevator. You gotta keep it *down*, let the goodies do their work, leave the gates of Heaven open, let that Senegalese Thunderfuck work its magic spell. (*Finally expelling air.*)

JIMMY. You're a regular poet.

VITO. (*Holding out joint to* JIMMY.) Yeah. Here, make daddy proud of you. Go on, go on . . . (JIMMY *takes a deep drag, holds it down for a second or two, then blows it out.*) Look, guy, you gotta—

JIMMY. Wait a minute, that was just a rehearsal. (*Walks to* c. *as* VITO *stashes baggie on shelf below;* JIMMY *takes a deep "toke" and holds it down.*)

VITO. That's a good boy. Good, hold it down now. Good! You're gonna get a *Gold Star*, and if you're extra good—you're gonna get to stay after school and do naughties with the teacher.

JIMMY. (*Exhaling in laughter.*) You're something else. (*Shrugs, looks at the joint, then at* VITO.) See— nothing?

VITO. (*Mischieviously.*) Wait . . .

JIMMY. (*Taking another puff.*) I've been wanting to ask you something. How come you only carry one bullet in your gun?

VITO. Oh, that's a buddy's gun, Jitter's. He carries one bullet for luck. I'm just keepin' it for him while he's in the slammer. See, Jitters, he calls his gun *Maurice*. I'll say, "Ey, wha'dja do last night, Jitters?" "Oh, me and Maurice went out to Long Island." Sometimes he don't even have a bullet. See, just the sight of a gun puts people off.

JIMMY. Yeah, I guess your average person— (*Stops*

dead, eyes wide, utters a low guttural.) Ohh . . . Wow . . . ! (*Steadies himself.*) I—I just got a—like a wave. (*Shakes his head.*) Oh, I think I feel it. (*Wobbling toward* VITO.) So soon?

VITO. Didn't I tell you? This stuff don't stall around. Hey, lemme see your eyes. (JIMMY *stares at him with eyes wide.*) You're on your way. Yeah, you're launched; your eyes look like Crazy Cat.

JIMMY. (*Heading back to the chaise.*) Wow—hey, don't *you* feel it?

VITO. Sure, but I'm used to it.

JIMMY. Whew— (*Sits.*) I'm really spinning. What time does this plane get to Omaha? Oh—oh, yeah, I know what I have to do.

VITO. What?

JIMMY. I have to sit down! (*Realizes he is sitting.*) Ooh, I'm losing my mind already.

VITO. Don't sweat it, you'll be fine.

JIMMY. Oh, I file feen. I mean—I feel fine. (*Getting a rush.*) Wow, Jesus, everything's coming out assbackwards. *I'm* backwards. (*Giggling.*) Okay, backwards, backwards! Hey, Vito, did you know "motel" spelled backwards is "let 'em?" (*Rising, walking to* c.) And ping-pong spelled backwards is "Ga-nip-ga-nop?" Not only that, did you know that air-raid spelled backwards is dia-rria?

VITO. Hey, you're not bad, once you get a head of steam up! Was you ever on Broadway?

JIMMY. Was I ever on Broadway! Five times! Yeah . . . five times in twenty years. First time, thank you very much, Aunt Claire dragged me by my fetlocks to my first audition. It was a huge Broadway musical. About the life and times of Carmen Miranda. There was this big hat scene. I played a grape! Ah-ah, but not just a grape—a *dancing* grape! Last time on Broadway, two years ago, major appearance. It's really great to be thirty-six years old and listed in the Playbill as

"Soldiers, Monks, Virgins, Bell-ringers and Hump-backs!"

VITO. Hey, I'd of liked to caught your act.

JIMMY. My act, my act! (*Doing quick tap dance.*) Kate was right—acting, what a tacky business!

VITO. How come? Everybody thinks it's—uh—glamorous.

JIMMY. Glamorous? You should have caught me auditioning for a commercial last week. Now, get this scene: nine men and three women glued together behind this long conference table, staring at me like they're producing, "War and Peace Meets Ben Hur," instead of a one-minute commercial for some new soft drink, "Squirt/Splash/Snatch"—something momentous like that. (*Giggles.*) Catch the director: (*Very pompous.*) "Mr. Zoole?—Zoole, is that—ah—your real name?" (*Aside to* VITO.) No—like I changed it for the stage, right? (*Then.*) Yes, it's my real name. (*The director again.*) "Mr. Zoole, here's our scene: You dive into a pool, swim the length, jump out, shake off the water, and our spokeswoman hands you the drink. You take a sip and say, "Wow, that's the most refreshing—what is it?" Only one line, but it's important. Think you can handle that?" (*To* VITO *again.*) Well, I don't know, I've only been in the business twenty years. Maybe I should start out with something simple like: "Da-da, goo-goo, kah-kah!" Yes, I think I can handle that. (*Back as the director.*) "Okay, Mr. Zoole, dive in!" (*To* VITO.) Dive in! He actually wants me to dive in! (JIMMY *howls with laughter.*) And what's even funnier—I did! Took off my shoes, stepped up on this sofa. (*Steps up on chaise.*) And I dive in. (*Dives off, and pantomimes swimming from* S. R. *to* S. L.) And I swim the length of the conference table. Up, out, shake it off. (*Shakes off imaginary water.*) And I'm just reaching for this non-existent can when the director says, "Wait-a-minute, Mr. Zoole, you didn't look as if you were *enjoying the swim!*" Oh, Christ, how I wanted to say: "No, you see, there was a little speck of shit in the pool, *you!*"

VITO. Why didn't you? I'd have said— (*Props himself up, indicates "this" with thumb toward general area of his groin.*) swim *this,* enjoy *this!*

JIMMY. But—see, actors don't . . . well, I didn't. You want the job. Glamorous? I got a million of 'em. A humiliation a minute. (*Smacking his hands together.*) I'd like to do an audition now. They'd see a swim— Christ, I'd do a swan dive and *clear* that conference table! Funny, know how I feel? I feel like confronting my enemies. (*Shadow boxing vigorously.*) No, it's more like confronting the *enemy* part of my friends. Yeah, that's it!

VITO. I don't get you. Like how?

JIMMY. Like saying to Claire, "Look, about your money, don't keep promising to leave it to me. Do me a favor, take it with you!" And then, to Kate: (*Moving slowly toward* U. S. *chaise, as if he were backing her up.*) "Look, Angel-bumps, you said I ought to come on in the real world more like I do when I'm screwing. Well, you ought to act more like you do when *you're* doing it: softer, gentler, more giving. And— (*Pantomimes slapping her back and forth across the face.*) *you really ought to swallow an opinion now and then!*"

VITO. Ben said, "Opinions are like assholes—everybody's got one."

JIMMY. (*Sits on chaise. Sotto:*) That's profound. Yeah, ahhh,—what I'd really like, I'd like to hole up someplace and *write my book.* See, Vito—

VITO. Hey—know what I'm gettin' a big wallop outta? We ain't foolin' ourselves with the big interview bit. (JIMMY *jumps up, goes to the cassette, turns it off.*) We're really talkin' turkey—like you know me. Hey, I'm gettin' a kick!

JIMMY. Yeah . . . I guess I am, too . . . *Ey, Vito!*

See—what it is, when I'm writing—I mean, everything just comes pouring out, how I feel, about anything—just spills out. With acting, there's just . . . (*As Frankenstein's monster, three steps* D. S. C.) always part of me holding back, afraid to let it all hang out.

VITO. I getcha. Like it's easier to do it on the paper than in person.

JIMMY. Yeah-h-h.

VITO. Hey, guy—could you just loosen this one rope here around my back? You're killing my kidneys.

JIMMY. Sure. (*Going to* VITO.) Why the hell didn't you say something? (*Loosening rope's knot.*) Ah-ah, don't try any tricks, though—or I'll fix you good.

VITO. Yeah—what would you do?

JIMMY. I don't know. Sell you to the gypsies!

VITO. Big deal. You'd have to pay *them*.

JIMMY. You don't mind putting yourself down, do you?

VITO. See, that's what Ben was going to do: Teach me to like myself. For the main reason, if you don't like what's going on inside yourself, not much chance you're going to dig what's going on with the rest of the crowd.

JIMMY. So . . . ah, what about this Ben? (*Sits on chaise.*) How did you hook up with him?

VITO. I could tell ya' a lot better if I had a little fuel, like an orange or an apple. My belly's disaster area.

JIMMY. Sure. (*Walking to desk, then back to* VITO *with an apple.*) Here you go.

VITO. Thanks. (*Biting the apple.*) See, when I left Marcy, I just sort of fell into hustlin'. After begging for it, I meet someone wants it so bad, they pay me. Not only that, I get doused with affection. Right away, I figure I'm onto a winner; I figure I stumbled into my life's work.

JIMMY. (*Walking toward chaise.*) Uhh, only with men?

VITO. Oh, no, men and women, don't make no difference. A lot of it was done for *company*. Serious, no cop-out. (JIMMY *sits*.) See, I'd just split with Dolores-from-Pasadena. Oh man, great legs and melons; an ass like two duck eggs in a napkin—but a face on her would back up a Chinese funeral! But sweet . . . Anyhow, I was puttin' in time as a waiter between hook-ups in Santa Monica. Ben come in with a party of eight one night. Well, I had banjo eyes for him right off, and I thought I was getting returns. Just to make sure—and sorta open negotiations—I dumped a cup of vichysoisse in his lap. Three days later, I'm takin' care of him and his house, on the beach, at Malibu, while he's beatin' his brains out designing this arts center—he was a big architect, Ben was, one of the *biggest*.

JIMMY. Were you with Ben—when he died?

VITO. Was I with him? Was I ever with him? Yeah . . . (*Then.*) Ben was at his drafting table all day. About five o'clock we took a swim, a trot on the beach, and there was this sunset goin' on, so spectacular it looked like a really rotten postcard. Unbelievable! We decided to make it. Well, it was wild. What with the sunset and all, it was wide-screen, stereo, panoramic sensurround! We zoomed up to Mars, shot over to Venus and hit Heaven head-on—Bammo! Rave reviews for everyone. Then, you know how you just lay there after a super-special one and try to uncross your eyes? After a while, I got up and I said, "I'll get a towel." "Okay," Ben said, "Get the little yellow one." There was this nice little yellow towel we kept in a drawer near the bed, but the laundry just come back and it was down the hall. I got up, went to the john, washed up, got the towel, and by the time I come back to the bedroom, the sunset had took a powder and the room was dark. I said his name, but he was asleep. So I figure to let him rest while I get dinner in the works. About seven o'clock, I fixed him a rum and diet cola and go back to the bedroom to wake him for the news on TV. "Hey, Ben," I said; no answer. I switched on the lights. (*Pause.*) He was lying on his back, those big brown eyes—wide open. I—I—then I touched him . . . He was already cold. (*A beat, then a small ironic laugh from* VITO.) Would you ever imagine those would be the last two things two people would say, "I'll get a towel." "Okay, get the little yellow one." (JIMMY *takes off his party hat. They remain silent for several moments.*) Eey . . . I got too heavy. I didn't mean it, okay?

JIMMY. And you went off the deep end, huh?

VITO. Talk about your spins, whoo! I took to the sewers. See, I been playin' with a bunch of rats, 'cause rats is who you meet in the sewer. So I got kicked outta my latest pad . . . and I was wondering— could I spend the night?

JIMMY. (*Laughing.*) Could you spend the night? (*Rises, walks toward* VITO.) You can't even go to the *bathroom!* Could you spend the—

VITO. Oh, I been meanin' to tell you, while you was in there shaving and—I already *did!*

JIMMY. (*They both laugh.*) You're somethin' else. Hey, I'm feeling light again. Boy, that stuff of yours just goes on and on, doesn't it? You know what? I don't mean to put you down, but I'm getting awful tired of looking at your ass. (*Walks to bathroom.*)

VITO. You unveiled it, not me!

JIMMY. (*From inside bathroom.*) I know, I know.

TRIO. (*Offstage* R.—*Singing:*) "*Should old acquaintance be forgot . . .*" (CARMINE, JANIE *and* BOBBY *enter.* CARMINE, *all in black, Spanish-style, black gaucho pants, black shirt, boots, cape, sombrero and tote bag;* JANIE *in long party dress and short cape;* BOBBY *is dressed in white garage mechanic's outfit, like jumpsuit, with flyer's helmet and goggles. All are*

high, stoned and happy. All three onstage now.)
Happy New Year, Jimmy Zoole!

(*As* JIMMY *enters from* U. S. L. *bathroom door with
   bathrobe, the* TRIO *suddenly see* VITO *strapped
   down bare-bottomed. This incongruous sight, especially in square-Jimmy's apartment, fills them
   at first with stunned surprise, then outright joy.
   They all laugh hysterically, then stop as:*)

CARMINE. (*Smacking his hands together.*) Why,
Jimmy—what a beautiful buffet!

JIMMY. Carmine, Janie! Oh, God, I forgot. Listen,
I really did. (*Going to* VITO *with robe, covering his
ass.*) I was just going to—

CARMINE. (*Moving quickly to* VITO.) No, no—leave
it! It's nifty raw. I dig steak tartar! (*Yanks robe off*
VITO, *then blows a party horn directly at* VITO'S *behind.*) Everybody *up!* Company's here.

JANIE. (*Walking over for a better view of* VITO.)
Yes—I really adore tushies, tushies are heaven!

BOBBY. (*Coming over for a good look, too.*) They
do make a statement, don't they? (*Slipping goggles
up on his helmet.*)

CARMINE. (*Walking to chaise, thowing robe down,
laughing.*) Ow! Oh, Jimmy, after all these years!

JANIE. (*Throwing her arms around* JIMMY.) Oh,
baby—*I'm so happy for you!* (*She spins him around;
this breaks them all up again.*)

VITO. (*Glancing back at his rear.*) The act's a hit!

JIMMY. (*Picking up robe from the chaise, going to
cover* VITO *again.*) Oh, this is really— Ah, Carmine,
this is a friend of mine. Vito.

CARMINE. (*Snatching robe, throwing it over to the
bed.*) A *friend?* I should hope a friend! And Vito,
these are two friends of mine. (*Indicating* JANIE.)
Janie. (*Indicating* BOBBY.) And Bobby. (*Throws his
cape on the bed.*) But not necessarily in that order.

JANIE. Happy New Year—Vito.

VITO. (*Tipping his party hat to* JANIE.) Happy New Year!

BOBBY. Ow, Vito, *you are lookin' good!*

CARMINE. Jimmy, you remember Bobby don't you?

JIMMY. Oh, yeah, right.

BOBBY. (*Taking a close look at* VITO'S *face.*) Hey, Carmine, check this guy out. We've seen him at that new bar down by the river!

CARMINE. (*Coming in for a close look.*) What? At the Ankle Strap. (*Takes* VITO'S *face in his hand, looks at it, then at his behind, then back at the face.*) Hmn, I remember the *face.* Sure, I remember you, Vito. Very busy. Cruising everything—dogs, cats, wallpaper, *doorknobs!* Sure. (JIMMY *goes to bed for the robe.*)

VITO. Yeah, I seen you, too. I also seen better drag on French poodles!

CARMINE. Well—snip, snip, *snip!*

JIMMY. (*Draping robe over* VITO *again.*) Listen, Carmine—this is wild. I really—I forgot I even—

CARMINE. (*Yanks robe off, drops it on the floor.*) Yeah, Janie gave me your message. Couldn't believe it. Still can't! Oh, Jimmy . . .

BOBBY. (*Crossing toward phone.*) We tried to phone a couple times. Busy, busy, busy.

CARMINE. (*Looks to the phone, sees it's off the hook.*) Ah-ah-ah, that's not nice, leave word, then take the phone off. (*Replaces the receiver.*) But then I guess you got lost in your work with young people!

JIMMY. No, Carmine, it's just that I forgot all about—

CARMINE. No sweat, here we are!

JANIE. (*Walking to* JIMMY.) Oh, darling, you don't have any ice cream, do you? I'd kill for some ice cream. I've got the gross munchies! (*Holding stomach.*)

JIMMY. I think there's some in the freezer.

JANIE. Oh, we love you! (*Holds her hands up, mak-*

ing little fluttery fingers at his face, speaks in bird-like voice.) Beedie-beedie-beedie! (*On her way to kitchen, does the same toward* VITO *as she passes him.*) Beedie-beedie-beedie!

CARMINE. Where's Kate?—asked Carmine suspiciously.

JIMMY. (*Laughing.*) Oh— Kate went to a party; I didn't feel like it.

CARMINE. She went without you, left you alone with tush tartar! (*Indicating* VITO.)

JIMMY. (*Quickly.*) Oh, she'll be back, she'll be right back.

CARMINE. (*Waving hands, mimicking* JIMMY.) "She'll be back, she'll be right back!"

JIMMY. Hey, you all want a drink?

CARMINE. No, no—we're not on the juice, Bruce! (*Going to the bed, lying down.*)

BOBBY. (*Floating around.*) We're on everything else but roller skates! Wheee!

JANIE. (*Coming from the refrigerator.*) Oh, my God— Bascom-Robbins! Mandarin-chocolate. Oh, heaven, heaven! It's thrillers all around.

BOBBY. (*Lying on his back on the chaise, kicking his feet in the air.*) Gimme! Gimme! Gimme! (JANIE *gives him a taste.*) Mmnnnn. (*To* JIMMY.) Hey, you haven't got any peanut butter maybe?

JIMMY. No, sorry. Say, Janie, what about your party? Shouldn't you all be getting back and . . .

CARMINE. (*Getting up from the bed.*) Nooooo, no, no.

JANIE. No, they wouldn't even know we were gone. God, what a crew!

BOBBY. (*Getting up, too.*) Too bad Bellevue doesn't have a pick-up service!

JANIE. (*Eating, going to* JIMMY.) Good old Stella's there, poor driven thing, still running around threatening suicide. I told her tonight: "Stella, for God's sake, why don't you put *zippers* in your wrists and stop bugging everybody?"

BOBBY. She did, too!

JANIE. (*To* JIMMY.) Want some?

JIMMY. Yeah, matter of fact I do. (*Sits on chaise.*)

JANIE. (*Feeding him a spoonful.*) Now, Jimmy, don't you get all blue about the play and— (*Kneeling down.*) Oh, yes, I heard they're tearing this building down, too. Well, there's one thing to remember about life, darling—it's only *temporary!*

CARMINE. (*Moves to the chaise, lies down* U. S. *of* JIMMY, *his legs straddling* JIMMY *where he sits, getting cozy.*) Ah, you are some fox, Jimmy Zoole. Foxy-woxy! All the time we worked together—you played it so square. Mr. Square. (BOBBY *comes over to sit on floor near them.*) "Clark Kent," we used to call him. (*Deep basso imitation of Clark Kent, making glasses with rounded thumb and fore-finger in front of his eyes.*) "Hello, there, Carmine!" And now, Jimmy, when you come out of the phone booth you really— I mean, charge!

BOBBY. Charge!

JANIE. I think it's heaven.

CARMINE. (*Behind* JIMMY *on chaise, playfully nudging him.*) Or were you swinging away all the time? Yeah, I bet you were. Fess up! (*Tickles* JIMMY.)

JIMMY. (*Laughing, pulling away.*) Carmine, stop it—stop! I'm ticklish, goddamit! This is—come on, actually I don't, I— (*Trying to get away, he takes an easy tumble off chaise, landing on throw pillows on the floor, center.*)

CARMINE. Don't what?

JIMMY. Swing— I don't!

CARMINE and BOBBY. (*Laughing, both get up, flapping their arms and circling about like big birds.*) He doesn't swing! He doesn't swing! He doesn't swing!

CARMINE. (*Indicating* VITO.) Well, uh, then—what's that? Asked the District Attorney. Don't tell me that's your normal everyday New Year's Eve Centerpiece?

JIMMY. Vito, tell 'em— I don't, do I?

VITO. No, he don't. Like you said, he's Mr. Square.

BOBBY. (*Laughing.*) *Would you look* at who's giving the testimonial!

CARMINE. Yeah, what were the two of you doing—having a little neighborhood Tupperware party?

JANIE. Oh, that's divine—let's all have a Tupperware party! Who'll we invite? (*Digging back into the ice cream.*) Oh, this is *heaven!*

JIMMY. (*Rising from the pillows.*) Oh, this just doesn't make sense at all . . .

CARMINE. (*Going to* JIMMY.) So, who has to make sense? (*Puts his arms around* JIMMY *and tries to kiss him.*) Happy New Year, Jimmy Zoole.

JIMMY. (*Wrenches away, quickly walks toward sink unit.*) Jesus! Carmine, you pig!

JANIE. (*Lightly, her attention still on the ice cream.*) You boys play nice now . . .

CARMINE. (*Suddenly angry.*) What the hell is this? You got a guy with his ass sticking up in the air, and I can't even *kiss* you! (*A furious strutting walk to* JIMMY.) What kind of shit is that? (JIMMY *picks up the bathrobe;* CARMINE, *after a pause, hits on an idea.*) Oh, Jimmy— I think I get it now. Should have known from the sink bit. Probably playing some dumb little master-slave number. Come on, Bobby—he wants to play rough.

JIMMY. (*As* BOBBY *gets up.*) I don't want to play at all. (*Throws robe over* VITO *as* CARMINE *gives him a playful punch in the shoulder.*)

VITO. (*As* JIMMY *moves* D. S. *to get away from* CARMINE.) Why don't you get Maurice to help you? He likes to play rough.

JIMMY. (*Confused.*) Maurice? (*Still moving away, as* CARMINE *continues to pursue him, shoving and tickling him.*) *Maurice?*

BOBBY. (*Closing in from the other side.*) Who's Maurice? Hey, you guys into three-sies? (*Shoves* JIMMY *back toward* CARMINE.)

JIMMY. (*As* CARMINE *shoves him back to* BOBBY.) No, honest, Carmine— I can explain. (BOBBY *shoves* JIMMY *again*.) See, he was hiding under the bed! Carmine—Vito's a burglar!

CARMINE. (*As* BOBBY *kneels on floor behind* JIMMY.) Oh, Christ, of course—cops and robbers! (*Pushes* JIMMY, *who falls backwards over* BOBBY.)

BOBBY. Sure, cops and robbers. (*He and* CARMINE *both grab* JIMMY *and pin him down by the throw-cushions.*)

JIMMY. (*Held down, but struggling.*) No, no—wait a minute! Jesus, I'm telling you. He was robbing me and I caught him and—

VITO. Took his *gun* away from him, dummy! (*Trying to clue* JIMMY *in.*) You need a *gun* to play cops and robbers . . . Jimmy!

JIMMY. (*Glancing around as he struggles on the floor.*) Oh, yeah—that's right.

CARMINE. And then you took his pants off . . .

JIMMY. No, I tied him up and then—I cut 'em off.

BOBBY. (*Delighted.*) Cut them off? *Fan-fucking-tastic!*

CARMINE. Jimmy, Jimmy—relax, it's two against one. (*They turn* JIMMY *over with his face into a pillow.*) There you go.

VITO. (*Slapping the flat of his hand on the sink, then a big laugh.*) Okay, okay, the gig's up, Jimmy. Hey, man—they gotcha, *just like you got me!* Serves you right, you prick!

CARMINE. (*Big, as all three turn to look at* VITO.) Ah-hah!

BOBBY. (*Big.*) Ah-hah!

JANIE. (*Small, almost a sigh.*) Ah-hah . . .

BOBBY. What happens next, Carmine?

VITO. (*Conning, hustling.*) Let me up, man, and I'll show ya'. Come on, Carmine, Bobby—it's only fair to let me have tit for tat with my buddy, the Big Actor. Whaddya say? Let's have a little party.

CARMINE. (*He and* BOBBY *still hold* JIMMY *down.*) I don't know, Jimmy-here doesn't look like he's got the right spirit.

VITO. Don't go by the way he looks. He's as full of shit as a three-pound robin! Hey, Carmine, you like a good show, don't you?

CARMINE. A good show? Yeah, who doesn't?

VITO. Yeah, well, let me up, man, and the show goes on! Besides, I know how to get Jimmy-boy started. See, we got a little thing we do with—Vick's-Vapo-Rub and a cantaloupe!

CARMINE. (*After a take.*) Vick's-Vapo-Rub and a cantaloupe?

BOBBY. (*To* JIMMY.) Hey, doesn't that smart, guy?

CARMINE. (*Expansive.*) What the hell, it's New Year's. I got Jimmy-boy. Let him up, Bobby!

BOBBY. (*Rising, walking toward* VITO.) Great, it looks like we're gonna have our Tupperware party after all.

JIMMY. (*Giving* CARMINE *an elbow in the gut.*) I'll show you a Tupperware party! (*Wrenching free, scrambling* U. S. *and jumping up on the bed where he left the gun earlier.*)

CARMINE. (*After* JIMMY, *as he dives for the gun.*) Bobby, get him!

VITO. (*Yelling.*) Atta-boy, Jimmy—get Maurice!

JIMMY. (*Standing on the* U. S. *end of bed, gun in hand.*) Get back! (*As* CARMINE *and* BOBBY *crowd him.*) What do you think this is—a banana split? *Get Back!* (BOBBY *scrambles* D. S., *grabs the hassock as a shield;* CARMINE *backs against wall.*) See, Carmine, we did have this little game of cops and robbers going. I was the cop. I like being the cop. I mean—*I dig it!* And now get the big scoop—you three diz-bombs are under arrest!

CARMINE. (*Taking a step toward the bed.*) Hey, what the hell kinda—

JIMMY. (*Wagging the gun at them.*) Ah-ah, back Spot! Down boy! See, I learned from this friend of mine, Jitters—that you can get more with a kind word and a gun . . . than you can with just a gun. So, the Unholy Three of you, out of here, back to your own party! (*Advancing on* CARMINE *as* BOBBY *and* JANIE *scramble toward the front door.*)

CARMINE. (*Not ready to give up.*) Now, wait a minute, Jimmy. Come on, we can—

JIMMY. (*Waving the gun in his face.*) You think I wouldn't use it? Try me!

VITO. (*Cowering, helping with the act.*) Oh, Jesus —don't get him started with the gun! You do and you'll be fartin' through a hole in your side!

BOBBY. Carmine, check the eyes. I think he's squirrely.

JIMMY. You got it, creepo! Out, nice and peaceful now.

BOBBY. Jesus, Carmine, I think the show's over!

JIMMY. (*As* CARMINE *makes a move toward him.*) You think it isn't loaded. (*Looks at the gun, then at him.*) Well, you're right, it isn't. (*Tosses the gun onto the bed.*) But *I* am! And I want you out of here. (CARMINE *starts to throw a punch at him;* JIMMY *catches his arm, twists it in an arm-lock, turns him around, applying pressure and walking him toward the door.*) See, Carmine, you're supposed to be a friend of mine, but you mortify a person and a person don't forget that. I don't want anybody in my apartment *ever again,* unless I want them here. Have you got that straight? So the three of you—hit the yellow brick road! (*He propels* CARMINE *out the front door, which* JANIE *has opened.*)

BOBBY. (*Looking after* CARMINE.) Now look what you've done! I don't get it, what did we do wrong?

JIMMY. (*Stamping his foot, sending* BOBBY *scooting out the door.*) Out! Out!

JANIE. (*Just starting out, pokes her head back in.*) Oh, darling, I saw some Sara Lee in your freezer and—

JIMMY. Out, Janie! (*She exits, then* CARMINE *steps back in, elegantly furious, hands on hips.*) Carmine, chop-chop, no exhaust. Or do you want to argue about it? Cause if you do, I got a knuckle sandwich with your name on it.

CARMINE. (*Huffy and outraged.*) My cape—*if you please!* (JIMMY *tosses his cape, which he catches.*) My sombrero! (JIMMY *tosses his hat at him.*) *And* my purse! (JIMMY *tosses his purse.*) Jimmy Zoole, I just plain don't understand you anymore. Happy-Fucking-New-Year. You bitch! (*He exits.*)

JIMMY. (*Stepping out into the hallway, shouting after them.*) And don't come back, no encores, no tricks. Remember the Monitor and the Merrimac—and all the other *frigates!* (*Shuts the door, laughing.*) Ey, Vito . . . (*Walking toward him.*) Vito, we pulled it off!

VITO. Oh, Jimmy, you gotta do something about your *friends!*

JIMMY. Whaddaya mean, I just did! (*They slap hands, one palm up, one palm down.*)

VITO. Hey, you did good!

JIMMY. (*Begins to untie* VITO.) Yeah, I did, didn't I? But you clued me in. Matter-of-fact, I think I was doin' an imitation a' you!

VITO. Yeah? I guess we work pretty good as a team.

JIMMY. Listen, level with me: Did you ever really monkey around with Vick's-Vapo-Rub and a cantaloupe?

VITO. Get outta here; I just made that up!

JIMMY. Beats figs and mice.

VITO. You're damned right!

JIMMY. (*Handing* VITO *the robe.*) There you go. Okay, Vito, fly away home.

VITO. (*Sighs at his freedom, then:*) Heyyyyy-ahhhh

I don't got a home. (*Sliding off sink.*) Oww, I'm stiff as Romeo's pecker. Oww . . . (*Putting on robe, stretching.*) Hey, let's have a little drink to celebrate, okay?

JIMMY. Why the hell not? (*Going to refrigerator for new bottle of champagne.*)

VITO. Hey, what was you thinking about when they were holding you down?

JIMMY. (*Opens bottle.*) Uhhh, "*I Want Out.*"

VITO. (*Getting two glasses from kitchen shelves.*) Well, that figures.

JIMMY. . . . of acting. (*Pours champagne.*)

VITO. . . . of acting?

JIMMY. (*A revelation.*) Yes, by God!

VITO. I never would have thought of that. Out of *acting?* I don't get the connection.

JIMMY. I don't either, but I think I've made a command decision.

VITO. (*Raising his glass in a toast.*) Here's to it. "Hail Mary, full of Grace, four balls, take a base!"

JIMMY. I know what it is—Vito, it has suddenly occurred to me tonight that I just might be in the wrong business! Wow, could I have been fooling myself for *twenty years?* That's no minor occurrence, that's a goddam earthquake! Can you imagine what it's like to be in a business twenty years—and never doing anything special in it? Well, my book was special and I know I can write it in my own special way. I'm tired of going around with my hand out, *begging* for permission to work. I want to get up in the morning and be my own boss. And that's exactly what I'm going to do. Vito, I have to be alone to figure out how I can work it. So, Happy New Year, drink up and—

VITO. Ey, I thought I was spending the night.

JIMMY. Vito, don't you understand, I—

VITO. (*Walking* U. S. *to the window.*) We had a goddam blizzard out!

JIMMY. You'll survive it, Vito. You're a survivor if I ever met one.

VITO. (*Turning, walking back to* JIMMY.) Hah-hah, I gotcha. I can't go—not tonight. I got no pants. New Year's Day, stores all closed, you gotta put me up.

(JIMMY *goes to the closet, gets a suit on a hanger and an old-fashioned pair of boxer shorts, very baggy.*)

JIMMY. (*Presenting them to* VITO.) Here, Vito, Happy New Year from me to you.

VITO. A whole suit? I only need the pants.

JIMMY. Take the suit, it's not exactly in style anyhow.

VITO. (*Sarcastic, putting "him on."*) Ohh, how can you *say* that!

JIMMY. Here, take these. (*Hands him the shorts.*)

VITO. (*Holding them out.*) Oh, thanks—very *racy!*

JIMMY. (*Fishing in his pocket for some money.*) Here, take some money for a hotel room.

VITO. No, I don't want any money from you.

JIMMY. You got to have some money.

VITO. So—I'll snatch a purse.

JIMMY. (*Following* VITO, *holding out bills.*) No, take it. Here's twelve dollars, I spent most of—

VITO. I ain't gonna take money from *you!*

JIMMY. (*Jamming the money into pocket of suit.*) Here, it's in here, you have to have some. (VITO *goes into the bathroom, shuts door. A beat, then* JIMMY *goes to the kitchen, gets a shopping bag. He puts the cat's scratching post and food bowl into the bag, picks up toy mouse with bell attached, jiggles bell.*) Bobby Seale . . . I'm gonna miss the hell out of you. You were a rat to leave me. You punctuated the end of a whole era, but I just wish you'd stuck around for the new one. (*Gently drops toy mouse into bag.*)

VITO. (*Charging out of the bathroom, dressed in* JIMMY'S *pants which are too big for him.*) Okay, *I got it! I got it!*

JIMMY. Christ, I hope it's not catching!

VITO. No, just do me a favor and listen! Look, I took the book, I fouled you up good, I know. Okay, you wanna write your book, how long would it take?

JIMMY. Vito!

VITO. *How long?*

JIMMY. Six, eight, ten months, but— (*Picks up* VITO's *pea-coat and holds it out to him.*) I've got to move, I've got to live, I've got to eat. Vito—

VITO. (*Gingerly tugs down sleeves of the jacket, which* JIMMY *still holds, as he gets ready to put it on.*) So, you gotta live at the Waldorf? (*Makes a pass at the sleeve, grazing it, missing it, walking away from the coat, which* JIMMY *still holds and looks at, slightly befuddled.*) I'm in with the minor Mafia, I can get us a good clean cheap apartment on the Lower East Side.

JIMMY. *Us?* You mean—*you and me? Together again?*

VITO. Okay, hah-hah.

JIMMY. Vito . . . (*Holding out coat once again.*)

VITO. Okay, okay. I'm talking about a railroad flat, so we'd each have our own room, don't worry! (*Going to* JIMMY, *putting one arm into coat-sleeve;* JIMMY *tries to help him with the other arm, but:*) It's okay, I got it, I got it. (*Walking away with one arm in the coat.*) Look, I hate to wait tables, I'd rather train fleas. But I'll sign on at one of those pissy East Side fruit restaurants where I'll make good tips. (*Still pacing with one arm in coat.*) And if I wanna pull in tips, I pull 'em in. I pay the rent, buy the eats, keep the place all douched up spic and span—all you gotta do is fly the fingers over the keys.

JIMMY. (*Trying to help* VITO *into other sleeve, but* VITO *swivels, walks away, leaving* JIMMY *once again holding the coat.*) Do you really see us as a winning team, eh, Vito?

VITO. What's to win, you won't win nothin', but you'll get your friggin' book written! You won't even have to cook. Did you know I'm a good cook?

JIMMY. (*Getting* VITO's *airline bag from the bed.*) No, I must have skipped that on your resumé.

VITO. Yeah, well, I am; I got sent to gourmet cooking school by Francine-from-Miami. Gorgeous red hair—and so sophisticated she drove her car with her *legs crossed.* And smoked *cigarettes* while she was bein' *shtupped.*

JIMMY. (*Tosses pea-jacket at* VITO's *chest, puts the airline bag on the sink unit.*) Vito, it just wouldn't work!

VITO. (*Dumps coat on sink.*) You won't even let me have my pride back for what I done, will you? Okay, I'll put it this way. I'm not doin' it for you, I'm doin' it for myself. (*Opens the airline bag, digs out a notebook.*) Here, look at this. (*Hands notebook to* JIMMY.) Ben's handwriting: lists for my reading and listening education. (*Paces the room.*) The way Ben put it—so, okay, be a card, be the life of the party. Great at twenty-six, twenty-seven, twenty-eight. But then you're gonna wake up one day and—flash, you're forty, the big Four-Oh. Then you're gonna find out that what you are is just a dumb stupid schmuck that everyone's tired of, *and* your line of chatter *and* the buns have fallen; you can only get your dauber up when the *moon's full.* And, suddenly, people ain't knockin' you down and draggin' you home for patti-cakes. *Look at me.* You called me an alley cat. Right on the button. You know what Ben said once? "You better find out what you want in life because, baby, that's exactly what you're gonna get." Well, I don't want what I had. Here . . . (*Goes to* JIMMY, *finds a place in the notebook, jabs it with his finger.*) Look at this, what I wrote down just last week, on Christmas day. (*Walks away from him.*) Go ahead, read it out loud.

JIMMY. "I been a freak act all my life. I want out of the side-show and into the main tent."

VITO. I want out of the freak show and into the main tent. Not bad, huh?

JIMMY. You really want to do something for me? (*Handing him the shopping bag and notebook.*) Take this down, throw it in the trash when you go. And say goodnight.

VITO. Great, I work out this whole plan—it goes over like a turd in a punchbowl. (*Puts the notebook down on the chaise, peers into the bag.*) Oh, the cat's— (*Walks to* JIMMY, *near the sink, puts the bag down.*) listen, keep 'em. I bet I could find another little kitty for you.

JIMMY. I don't want a cat.

VITO. You liked your cat—

JIMMY. I liked my cat because he kept hanging around my door. He finally just moved in. I liked him, I loved *that* cat, but I don't like cats in general.

VITO. Okay, okay—what about a dog? I'll bet I could find you a cute little puppy?

JIMMY. Why, you know a pet shop you can knock off?

VITO. Come on, guy. Level with me, and tell me why you're dumpin' cold water on my plan?

JIMMY. (*Picks up bag, coat, goes to* VITO, *taking him by the arm and dragging him toward the front door.*) Vito, it's just too wild, that's all.

VITO. Wild? (*Stopping dead.*) What's wrong with that? Wild for a writer should be good. Okay, wild . . . wild! (*Breaking away, dashing back to* c. *of the room.*) Okay, wild, wild. *Wild*—look at Grace Kelly!

JIMMY. (*Amazed.*) *Grace Kelly!*

VITO. Yeah, Grace Kelly. She started out a poor little pussy from Pittsburgh . . .

JIMMY. Philadelphia . . .

VITO. Philadelphia-Pittsburgh. Big deal . . .

JIMMY. And she was rich to begin with . . .

VITO. Okay, she's still a little pussy from Philadelphia, and now she's a goddam Princess.

JIMMY. She was already a big fat movie star!

VITO. Okay, okay, *forget Grace Kelly!*

JIMMY. (*A threatening step toward* VITO.) *Vito!*

VITO. (*Turning away, walking* U. S. C.) Boy, you can't win with you! (*Looks out window.*) Hey, you don't got a pair of skis, do you?

JIMMY. *Vito, I'm not going to say it again.*

VITO. Okay, I'm going. (*Gets his coat and the bags, walks to the front door as* JIMMY *follows a few steps behind.*) Well, goodnight. (*He sets the bags on the floor, examines the coat for lint, picks off a piece or two, still stalling.*) Maybe we'll crash into each other again sometime.

JIMMY. Maybe we will, maybe.

VITO. Wanna bet we will? (*Buttoning coat.*)

JIMMY. You're too much, Vito Antonucci.

VITO. Likewise, Jimmy Zoole. (*Picks up bags, quickly puts them down.*) Hey, listen—oh—I left you the thunderfuck . . . (*On his way into the room.*)

JIMMY. (*Intercepting him, pushing him back toward door.*) Thanks. Thank you.

VITO. (*Putting on his knitted cap.*) Listen, what the hell—we put in New Year's together. Would it be okay if I call or—drop by sometime? Just for old times' sake?

JIMMY. (*Laughing.*) Sure. So long, Vito. Happy Hunting.

VITO. Oh, yeah, uh, Happy New Year. (*Goes to give* JIMMY *a quick embrace, which* JIMMY *blocks.* VITO *quickly assumes a heavy jock attitude, hitching up his pants, smacking one fist into the other.*) Oh, that's right, I forgot, we're still playin' lumberjacks. (*Smacks fist again.*) Pow! Bang! Vop! So long, Mac, don't take any wooden nickels. (*Gathering up his things.*) And—ah—whatever you do, don't take any chances. One of 'em might work out. (*Opens door, does blizzard imitation, "fighting the raging winds," almost falling backwards.*) Whooooosh! . . . Whoooo! . . . Phewwwwww! (JIMMY *braces him, finally shoves him out the door and closes it.* JIMMY *remains at the door for a moment, smiling, then walks to the window, opens it, and gets a blast of cold air in his face.)*

JIMMY. Geeez, freezing! *(Runs to the door, starts to open it, then catches himself, shakes his head.)* Oh, no. No, no. When thy cup runneth over—looketh out! *(Crosses* D. S. *to the chaise, notices the notebook* VITO's *left behind, picks it up and reads:)* "Art is easy, it's life that's the bitch!" . . . "I asked Ben if he thought there was an afterlife. His answer: What, after all this horseshit, if there isn't—it's a goddam swindle!" *(Grinning,* JIMMY *closes the book, stretches and walks toward the bathroom. He catches sight of himself in the mirror as he's passing.)* Happy New Year, Jimmy Zoole! *(Exits into the bathroom.* VITO *is seen outside the skylight, peering down. The coast is clear; he pries it open again. He drops his airline bag onto the bed, then drops himself down after it.* VITO *glances toward the bathroom, then quickly and quietly scoots into the kitchen, putting his airline bag down, opening the refrigerator and taking out a chicken leg, picks up the garlic seasoning from counter. He walks to the sink unit, perches atop it, munching the chicken leg which he liberally sprinkles with garlic powder.* JIMMY's *Voice—heard from the bathroom as* VITO *opens refrigerator.)* I'll work it out, I will. I will not be lonely; I will not be depressed. New York is *fun* in Winter. New York is a *Winter Festival.* This is a recording.

VITO. *(Calling out.)* Ah-ah, six years in solitary for talkin' to yourself!

JIMMY. *(Rushing out of bathroom in pajamas.)* Jesus—*Vito*—what are you doing here?

VITO. You said I could drop in sometime, so I dropped in!

JIMMY. Oh, Vito—everything in excess! Everything!

VITO. It's cold as a polar bear's balls out!

JIMMY. All right, all right! The Zoole Hilton extends its hospitality for one night— (*Going to closet, getting sheet and blanket.*) But one night only, *do you understand?* Is it a deal? (*Walking toward* VITO.)

VITO. It's a deal. You're a prince. (*Taking off coat, leaving it on sink unit.*)

JIMMY. And you're a . . . No, there's got to be a new word invented for you! (*Handing the bedding to him.*) Vito, I know you'll find this hard to believe, but this night is over, it's had it, it's dead as a duck. No more talk, no more horseplay—nothing but bed and sleep. Have you got that through your thick, persistent, petrified skull? (*Going to chaise, clearing it of phone etc., so* VITO *can make it up into a bed.*)

VITO. Yes. Yeah, okay. Wow, what do you know, they found Martin Boorman alive and well and living right here in Greenwich Village. (JIMMY *walks toward front door, switches ENTRANCE LIGHTS OFF.* VITO *going to chaise, with bedding.*) And wouldn't you wear pee-jays! You probably wear one of those hats with a little ball and tassle . . .

JIMMY. (*Walking to sink.*) Goodnight, *and amen.*

VITO. (*Making up his bed on chaise.*) We'll give my idea another spin in the morning.

JIMMY. No, we won't. Goodnight! (*Tidying up sink area, folding* VITO'S *coat, etc.*)

VITO. It's a goddam good idea! I'd be helping you, and you'd be helping me.

JIMMY. Vito, let me ask you a question.

VITO. (*Beginning to strip to his undershirt and boxer shorts.*) Shoot.

JIMMY. Why don't you help yourself? You know, take a job as a waiter, get your own pad, get into reading and listening to good music; take some courses at NYU or whatever. Why don't you pull yourself together and do it on your own?

VITO. For the main reason, *it just don't mean nothin' to me, by myself.*

JIMMY. Vito, we've each got to pull our own act together; that's why we're here.

VITO. I'm just not a loner. That's the way I am.

JIMMY. Then you're a fool.

VITO. Let me ask *you* a question?

JIMMY. Make it good, because it's your last.

VITO. You had any better offers today?

JIMMY. No . . .

VITO. Then *you're* a fool.

JIMMY. (*Sotto.*) Goodnight. (*He turns KITCHEN LIGHTS OFF.*)

VITO. (*Sotto.*) Goodnight. (*He crawls under blanket on chaise. JIMMY goes to his bed, and gets under covers. VITO—after a long silence.*) I wish I had my fuckin' Teddy bear. (*A beat.*) Or something to keep me warm.

JIMMY. (*From bed.*) Vito, don't you ever give up?

VITO. Hardly ever, Jimmy-baby. Winners never quit and quitters never win. (*Rises and wraps blanket around shoulders, walks to lightswitch U. S. of sink.*) For the main reason— (*VITO switches KITCHEN LIGHTS ON.*) I can go on pretending I don't got arms, just as long as you can go on pretending *you* don't got arms. (*Pours himself a glass of champagne.*) You got my theme?

JIMMY. (*In bed.*) Theme—yeah, I got your theme. (*Pause.*) Theme!? (*Jumping out of bed, rushing to stool for his cassette.*) My God, have I got a theme.— Oh, have I!

VITO. What's a' matter, your spansule just go off?

JIMMY. (*Pacing excitedly.*) Yes, I think it did. When I was washing up, I was wondering why I'd been having so much trouble getting back into my book. The trouble is—I'd already written *that* book. It would be like having to recreate it all over again. Boring! But it just hit me. What about today, tonight, all that's happened? You. Me. The whole . . . Oh, Vito, do I have a now-book on my hands! (*Facing VITO.*) And I have you to thank for it. You think I don't got arms? (*Starts to embrace VITO, hesitates, then steps forward, gives VITO a quick hug, steps quickly back*

away from him as if he'd just won a battle.) Think
again. They're always saying you should write from
life. Well, I got a life, and that's what I'm going to do!

VITO. So you're going to write a book about *me?*

JIMMY. Hey, hey, I'm in it, too.

VITO. (*Puts down his glass on sink.*) Wel-l-l-l, this
now-book, about us, how's it gonna end?

JIMMY. Give me time, I have to think it out.

VITO. I bet I could come up with an ending that
would be gangbusters!

JIMMY. Hold it. I'm way ahead of you. Vito, you've
been pushing very hard. Isn't it funny how I noticed
that? Look, I've never made it with a guy, because
I've never really had the urge. But there are a whole
lot of changes taking place in my life, and if I ever
decide to give it a try—I'll be the first to let you
know.

VITO. You would?

JIMMY. Yes, I would. 'Cause you give me a kick,
you do. I clue in to you as a friend.

VITO. Yeah, well . . . just suppose you decide—
I mean like on a special occasion, say New Year's,
when you had one hell-of-a-day, and you got a lot
of new ideas rattlin' around up in your attic— (*Quietly
edging up to the bed, sitting, trying it out for size and
comfort.*) and because of all this, say you couldn't
sleep, and after a while you got lonesome. But you
was embarrassed to say anything—you could probably sneeze a couple of times, or cough loud, or drop
a shoe. And I'd probably get the idea.

JIMMY. (*Turning, see's* VITO *on bed, goes to him,
lifts him up by the "lapels" of the blanket and leads
him* D. S. *to chaise.*) Vito, if that should ever happen,
I think I'd better open up direct communications. See,
I have Hay Fever, and I tend to wake up in the
middle of the night sneezing. And we wouldn't want
to get our signals crossed. (*Walking to the sink.*) In
the meantime, it's nice to have company tonight. I'm

glad you dropped in, Vito. (*He turns KITCHEN LIGHTS OFF.*)

VITO. My pleasure. (*Lies down; JIMMY goes to his own bed and crawls in, then:*) Hey . . . would it be okay if I say my prayers before I go to sleep?

JIMMY. (*Near the end of his patience.*) If they're short!

VITO. They're short. (*Clears throat.*)

    The Lord is my Shepherd

    He knows what I want . . .

JIMMY. (*After a long pause, sitting up in bed. Sotto.*) Hey . . . ! Vito . . . !

VITO. (*Sits up too. Sotto.*) Yeah, guy?

JIMMY. (*Good humoredly, warm, a loud whisper.*) Blow-it-out-your-*ass!*

BLACKOUT—END OF ACT TWO

PROPERTY PLOT

Act One—Off s. r.:

Upstairs—
  bag—(Jimmy's)
    2 bottles champagne
    1 jar pickles
    1 delicatessen wrap turkey
    1 cole slaw
    party bag
      2 paper hats
      2 horns
    horn (Bobby's)
    whistle (Carmine's)
    pitcher water
    cape and bag (Carmine's)
    suitcase (Kate)

Personal—s. l.:

Vito's bag
  gun with blank
  note book
  marijuana—2 joints
  flashlite
  screw driver

Kate
  keys
  letter

Check window is closed

Closet s. r.—
  blue blanket
  brown sheet
  costumes
    fur coat
    smoking jacket (Jimmy)
    suit and underpants (Vito)

Stereo area—
  Harris album

Chaise—
  brown pillow

Table Next to Chaise—
  vase with flowers
  lighter and cigarettes (True Blues)
  ashtray with water
Bed—
  make up per show
  slippers (D. S. R. end under)
  glass of water (D. S. R. end—Vito)
Bed Bench
  magazines
  TV S. L.—cord short
Desk—
  cassette
  script
  desk lamp
  tree
  waste basket (S. R.)
  typewriter case (S. L.)
  chair (radiator under)
  top drawer
    camera
    scissors
Bathroom Wall Shelf—
  practical saucer (second to bottom shelf)
  stool (nest under)
Sink—Add Water Daily
  fruit bowl with fruit
  telephone and pen and pad (below)
  rope presets
  towel ring and towel
  scotch bottle with liquid (U. S. end)
  set dressing bottles (U. S. end)
  broom (U. S. at pillar)
  pan *on* pillar
Kitchen Shelves—
  second—from top
    vase
    2 candles (check wicks)
    ginger jar
    4 rock glasses
  third—
    3 champagne glasses

under—
   scratch post
   waste basket and dust pan
   butler stand and tray (near refrigerator, **folded**)
Refrigerator—
  ice bucket (on top D. S. **end**)
  inside
    cat food can
    bowl of pudding
    chicken leg
    ice cream (in freezer)
    ice (in freezer)
    mayonnaise
    plastic vegetables, assorted
Stove—
  kettle on top
  pots and pans on rack above
    Vito's pot—third hook from D. S.
Butcher block float unit—
  cookie jar with cookies
  salt, pepper, and garlic
  matches
  shelf (in float unit)
    plate
    silverware—knife, fork, and 3 spoons
    place mat
    napkin
  bottom shelf (float unit)
    rope
    shopping bag
  S. R. side of float unit
    double cat food bowl
    toy mouse with belltail
Run Area
  hassock (lined up with bed and **sink, on c. line**)
  brown and blue pillows, (D. S. L.)
For Consumption:
  2 bottles of champagne
  1 bottle of whiskey
  1 jar of pickles
  1 deli-wrap turkey

1 container cole slaw
cookies
ice cubes
1 Baskin-Robbins ice cream serving
water in sink pump
cat food bowl—tapioca (refrigerator)
mayonnaise jar—vanilla yogurt (refrigerator)
drinking water Off S. R.
drinking water under bed (Vito)
apple (set in fruit bowl for Act Two only)
fresh flowers (table, S. R.)
2 joints (Bidi tobacco rolled as marijuana)
Bathroom (*Off* S. L.)—Over Sink:
  brown bath towel
  brown washcloth
  brown hand towel
KATE—S. R. side:
  brush
  comb
  toothbrush
First Prop Table:
  makeup case (Kate)
  makeup bag (Kate)
  assorted cans, bottles, cosmetics (Kate)
  blue negligee (Kate)
  blue nightgown (Kate)
  diaphragm case (Jimmy)—on R. side of sink
Rear Prop Table:
  money—$12.00 (Jimmy)
  keyring (Jimmy)
  "Habit Rouge" bottle (Jimmy)
  brown hand towel (Jimmy)
  champagne glass (filled)—(Jimmy)
  pajamas (Jimmy)
  blue robe (Jimmy)
  black peacoat (Vito)
  knit cap (Vito)
Act Two:
  pick up torn letter U. S. C.
  plug in TV set and extend cord
  telephone to chaise

Vito's coat—to bed
flightbag—D. S. L. corner of bed (unhook from underbed
  hook—unzipper and double-check dope)
gun between pillows on bed
strike album
Party Decorations—hang about set:
  2 streamers
  5 spirals
Kitchen:
  strike butler tray, dishes, and silver
  strike broom to bathroom door corner
  2 champagne bottles
    1 on float unit
    1 in refrigerator
  mouse—S. R. of float counter
  party bag—under kitchen shelves
  strike used glasses
  shopping bag under float counter
  flashcube in camera, top desk drawer—(must have four un-
    used bulbs—two are standby)

NOTE: To insure Vito's maximum comfort being strapped
down, there should be a hunk of foam rubber put in the well
of the sink to support him during the change after Scene 1,
Act One. It is also wise to line the edges of the sink over which
his feet hang with foam rubber covered in silver masking tape
or whatever color tape the sink is, to prevent his shins from
being bruised when he struggles. The straps tying him down
should look like home-made combinations of rope, belts,
neckties etc. for reality's sake. Solid hooks should be placed
under the lips of the sink on both sides so these straps can
be fastened and unfastened quickly during scene changes to
allow Vito to escape quickly and get back in place in the
event there is no curtain but only a blackout to work in.
These changes should be rehearsed by the stage crew so they
can be accomplished in the minimum amount of time.

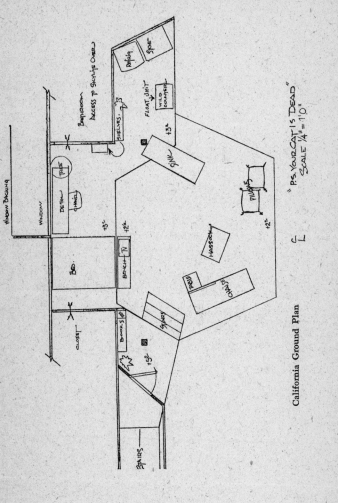

California Ground Plan

"P.S. YOUR CAT IS DEAD"
SCALE 1/4" = 1'0"

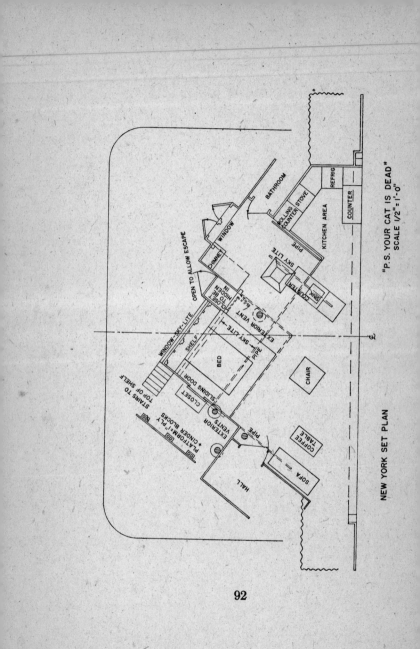

"P.S. YOUR CAT IS DEAD"
SCALE 1/2" = 1'-0"

NEW YORK SET PLAN

92

HERE'S HOW

A Basic Stagecraft Book

THOROUGHLY REVISED
AND ENLARGED

by HERBERT V. HAKE

COVERING 59 topics on the essentials of stagecraft (13 of them brand new). *Here's How* meets a very real need in the educational theater. It gives to directors and others concerned with the technical aspects of play production a complete and graphic explanation of ways of handling fundamental stagecraft problems.

The book is exceptional on several counts. It not only treats every topic thoroughly, but does so in an easy-to-read style every layman can understand. Most important, it is prepared in such a way that for every topic there is a facing page of illustrations (original drawings and photographs)—thus giving the reader a complete graphic presentation of the topic along with the textual description of the topic.

Because of the large type, the large size of the pages (9″ x 12″), and the flexible metal binding, *Here's How* will lie flat when opened and can be laid on a workbench for a director to read while in a *standing* position.

#104

VERONICA'S ROOM
IRA LEVIN
(Little Theatre) Mystery
2 Men, 2 Women, Interior

VERONICA'S ROOM is, in the words of one reviewer, "a chew-up-your-finger-nails thriller-chiller" in which "reality and fantasy are entwined in a totally absorbing spider web of who's-doing-what-to-whom." The heroine of the play is 20-year-old Susan Kerner, a Boston University student who, while dining in a restaurant with Larry Eastwood, a young lawyer, is accosted by a charming elderly Irish couple, Maureen and John Mackey (played on Broadway by Eileen Heckart and Arthur Kennedy). These two are overwhelmed by Susan's almost identical resemblance to Veronica Brabissant, a long-dead daughter of the family for whom they work. Susan and Larry accompany the Mackeys to the Brabissant mansion to see a picture of Veronica, and there, in Veronica's room, which has been preserved as a shrine to her memory, Susan is induced to impersonate Veronica for a few minutes in order to solace the only surviving Brabissant, Veronica's addled sister who lives in the past and believes that Veronica is alive and angry with her. "Just say you're not angry with her," Mrs. Mackey instructs Susan. "It'll be such a blessin' for her!" But once Susan is dressed in Veronica's clothes, and Larry has been escorted downstairs by the Mackeys, Susan finds herself locked in the room and locked in the role of Veronica. Or is she really Veronica, in the year 1935, pretending to be an imaginary Susan?

> The play's twists and turns are, in the words of another critic, "like finding yourself trapped in someone else's nightmare," and "the climax is as jarring as it is surprising." "Neat and elegant thriller."—*Village Voice.*

ROYALTY, $50–$35

MY FAT FRIEND
CHARLES LAURENCE
(Little Theatre) Comedy
3 Men, 1 Woman, Interior

Vicky, who runs a bookshop in Hampstead, is a heavyweight. Inevitably she suffers, good-humouredly enough, the slings and arrows of the two characters who share the flat over the shop; a somewhat glum Scottish youth who works in an au pair capacity, and her lodger, a not-so-young homosexual. When a customer—a handsome bronzed man of thirty—seems attracted to her she resolves she will slim by hook or by crook. Aided by her two friends, hard exercise, diet and a graph, she manages to reduce to a stream-lined version of her former self—only to find that it was her rotundity that attracted the handsome book-buyer in the first place. When, on his return, he finds himself confronted by a sylph his disappointment is only too apparent. The newly slim Vicky is left alone once more, to be consoled (up to a point) by her effeminate lodger.

> "My fat Friend is abundant with laughs."—*Times Newsmagazine.* "If you want to laugh go."—*WCBS-TV.*

ROYALTY, $50–$35

THE GOOD DOCTOR
NEIL SIMON

(All Groups) Comedy
2 Men, 3 Women. Various settings.

With Christopher Plummer in the role of the Writer, we are introduced to a composite of Neil Simon and Anton Chekhov, from whose short stories Simon adapted the capital vignettes of this collection. Frances Sternhagen played, among other parts, that of a harridan who storms a bank and upbraids the manager for his gout and lack of money. A father takes his son to a house where he will be initiated into the mysteries of sex, only to relent at the last moment, and leave the boy more perplexed than ever. In another sketch a crafty seducer goes to work on a wedded woman, only to realize that the woman has been in command from the first overture. Let us not forget the classic tale of a man who offers to drown himself for three rubles. The stories are droll, the portraits affectionate, the humor infectious, and the fun unending.

"As smoothly polished a piece of work as we're likely to see all season."—*N.Y. Daily News.* "A great deal of warmth and humor —vaudevillian humor—in his retelling of these Chekhovian tales."—*Newhouse Newspapers.* "There is much fun here . . . Mr. Simon's comic fancy is admirable."—*N.Y. Times.*

$1.75 (Music available. Write for particulars.)
ROYALTY, $50–$35

The Prisoner of Second Avenue
NEIL SIMON

(All Groups) Comedy
2 Men, 4 Women, Interior

Mel is a well-paid executive of a fancy New York company which has suddenly hit the skids and started to pare the payroll. Anxiety doesn't help; Mel, too, gets the ax. His wife takes a job to tide them over, then she too is sacked. As if this weren't enough, Mel is fighting a losing battle with the very environs of life. Polluted air is killing everything that grows on his terrace; the walls of the high-rise apartment are paper-thin, so that the private lives of a pair of German stewardesses next door are open books to him; the apartment is burgled, and his psychiatrist dies with $23,000 of his money. Mel does the only thing left for him to do: he has a nervous breakdown. It is on recovery that we come to esteem him all the more. For Mel and his wife and people like them have the resilience, the grit to survive.

"Now all this, mind you, is presented primarily in humorous terms."—*N.Y. Daily News.* "A gift for taking a grave subject and, without losing sight of its basic seriousness, treating it with hearty but sympathetic humor . . . A talent for writing a wonderfully funny line . . . full of humor and intelligence . . . Fine fun."—*N.Y. Post.* "Creates an atmosphere of casual cataclysm, and everyday urban purgatory of copelessness from which laughter seems to be released like vapor from the city's manholes."—*Time.*

$1.75. ROYALTY, $50–$35

Witness for the Prosecution

Melodrama—3 Acts

By AGATHA CHRISTIE

17 Men, 5 Women. Interior—Modern Costumes

Winner of New York Critics Circle Award and the Antoinette Perry Award. One of the greatest mystery melodramas in years.
The story is that of a likable young drifter who is suspected of bashing in the head of a middle-aged, wealthy spinster who has willed her tidy estate to him. His only alibi is the word of his wife, a queer customer, indeed, who, in the dock, repudiates the alibi and charges him with the murder. Then a mystery woman appears with damaging letters against the wife and the young man is freed. We learn, however, that the mystery woman is actually the wife, who has perjured herself because she felt direct testimony for her husband would not have freed him. But when the young man turns his back on his wife for another woman, we realize he really was the murderer. Then Miss Christie gives us a triple-flip ending that leaves the audience gasping, while serving up justice to the young man.

(ROYALTY, $50-$25.)

The Mousetrap

The longest-run straight play in London history.

Melodrama—3 Acts

By AGATHA CHRISTIE

5 Men, 3 Women—Interior

The author of Ten Little Indians and Witness for the Prosecution comes forth with another English hit.
About a group of strangers stranded in a boarding house during a snow storm, one of whom is a murderer. The suspects include the newly married couple who run the house, a spinster, an architect, a retired Army major, a strange little man who claims his car overturned in a drift, and a feminine jurist. Into their midst comes a policeman, traveling on skiis. He no sooner arrives than the jurist is killed. To get to the rationale of the murderer's pattern, the policeman probes the background of everyone present, and rattles a lot of skeletons. Another famous Agatha Christie switch finish! Chalk up another superb intrigue for the foremost mystery writer of her half century. Posters and publicity.

(ROYALTY, $50-$25.)